MW01231831

Ministering Hope
to the Hurting Heart:
a Guide for Christians

Roberta Fish, LCSW

Dear Alison,
I pray you
have many blessings
on your life journey!
Love, Roberta

XULON PRESS

Copyright © 2013 by Roberta Fish

Ministering Hope to the Hurting Heart:
a Guide for Christians
by Roberta Fish

Printed in the United States of America

ISBN 9781625093219

All rights reserved solely by the author. The author guarantees all contents are original and do not infringe upon the legal rights of any other person or work. No part of this book may be reproduced in any form without the permission of the author. The views expressed in this book are not necessarily those of the publisher.

Unless otherwise indicated, Bible quotations are taken from The New King James Version of the Bible. Copyright © 1976 by Thomas Nelson, Inc; The New American Standard Bible (NASB). Copyright © 1995 by The Lockman Foundation; The New International Version (NIV). Copyright © 1984 by Biblica Publishing; The New Living Translation (NLT). Copyright © 2007 by Tyndale House Foundation; The New Revised Standard Version (NRSV). Copyright © 1989 by the National Council of the Churches of Christ and The Message (Message). Copyright © 2002 by NavPres.

www.xulonpress.com

Dedicated to

My Great Healer, Jesus Christ
My best friend and encourager, my husband, Howard Fish
My partner in *Hope for Hurting Hearts* – Juanita Mayer-Bartel
My best teachers - my clients and students

Table of Contents

Chapter 1

Introduction

W endy walked through life feeling dead and alone; she knew something was wrong. She longed to feel love for God, her husband and her children the way others experienced it. She believed she was defective through and through; shame was her daily companion. She couldn't follow good health principles and indulged in junk food secretly and regularly. Her husband was unkind to her, but she saw this as normal and justified. She suffered from frightening dreams and nightmares about blood and violence. These reinforced her belief that she was bad, maybe even demon-possessed. Wendy tried many things in an attempt to feel alive, but sometimes she felt so unworthy of love, she hurt herself. To her way of thinking, she was getting what she deserved. She kept everyone at arm's length. If people really knew her, Wendy thought, they would know what a terrible person she was.

Wendy had been emotionally abused by her mother, physically abused by her father and sexually abused by a church school teacher and pastor. The church school teacher and pastor also abused her spiritually because of their positions of trust. She knew what happened was wrong and she tried to talk to her mother about it once. Her mother told her to just stay away from them. She tried, but it didn't work and she blamed herself for being unable to avoid the abuse. She talked about it to another teacher and the teacher told the school board chairman. The school board met about it, but the teacher, unbelievably, stayed there two more years and continued abusing Wendy. That was the last time she tried to tell anyone.

I wish I could tell you that this is a made-up story. It is not. And this story is repeated every day in countless families and churches. Abuse is a heart-breaking epidemic with far-reaching consequences.

- Every year nearly one million children are victims of physical abuse.[1] In the U.S. five children die every day from abuse injuries.[2] If there were retrospective studies about adults who were physically abused as children, the numbers would be staggering.
- Adult retrospective studies show that 25-40% of women and 10-15% of men were sexually abused before the age of 18.[3] This means there are more than 42 million adult survivors of child sexual abuse in the U.S, and the statistics are similar in the church population. This statistic is about *reported* cases. The levels are actually higher because 73% of child victims do not tell anyone about the abuse for at least a year. 45% of victims do not tell anyone for at least five years and the majority never disclose.[4]
- One in four women is experiencing or has experienced domestic violence.[5] An estimated 1.3 million women are victims of physical assault by an intimate partner each year.[6] Ninety percent of domestic violence victims are women.[7] Most cases of domestic violence are never reported to the police.[8] Studies suggest that between 3.5 - 10 million children witness some form of domestic violence annually.[9]
- There is very little research showing rates of emotional abuse, neglect and abandonment (unless severe which comes under physical abuse statistics).
- Spiritual abuse has no accountability office that keeps track. These abuses do happen frequently; they're just not documented.

All these statistics show that large numbers of hurting hearts live in our communities, churches and families. Recovery from abuse is a difficult process; a painful and confusing journey. The ministry of healing to survivors is so necessary and vital on this rocky road to restoration.

As we think of abuse, questions bombard us and we wonder:

- How could abuse that happened years ago still affect someone today?
- What does real healing look like?
- How long will it take?
- What are the different stages of healing?
- What about the abusers, do they need healing?
- Is healing even possible?
- Where is God in all this?

Seventeen years ago, Juanita Mayer-Bartel, chaplain at Shawnee Mission Hospital, and I created Hope for Hurting Hearts, an educational supportive week-end for abuse survivors. (www.hopeforhurtinghearts.com) Our goal was to give survivors a vision of healing and instill hope as they journeyed through the process. Hope for Hurting Hearts retreats have taken place numerous times across North America and this book is a natural extension of that ministry. As you journey through this book you will gain hope, a vision of the healing journey and the knowledge to support survivors as they heal. As you acquire an understanding of the big picture, you will be empowered to minister hope to the hurting heart.

When speaking of those who have been abused the term "survivor", as opposed to "victim", will be used throughout the book. It's true that those who were abused are victims; a victim is defined as "someone who is harmed or killed by another, someone who is harmed by or made to suffer from an act, circumstance, agency, or condition, a person who is tricked, swindled, or taken advantage of."[10] But, the abused are so much more. In my thirty years as a therapist, I have seen people who have suffered horrendous abuse embody the definition of the word survivor: one who "remains alive, carries on despite hardships or trauma and remains functional."[11] Those who have endured abuse have been in a terrible war and I greatly respect their courage and creativity. Yes, they are survivors in every sense of the word.

Addressing healing from *childhood* abuse is the major focus of this book. However, the healing process described is also applicable to *adult* abuse. Appendix VII about Domestic Violence and Appendix VIII about Sexual Assault address some specific information on adult abuse.

Almost all of us have had a physical wound at some time in our life. That experience assists us in identifying and understanding the process of healing. We'll answer the following questions applying what we know about a physical wound to healing the wounds of abuse:

1. How are people wounded? (Chapter 3)
2. What are the effects of being wounded? (Chapter 4)
3. What is the first stage of healing? (Chapter 5)
4. What is the second stage of healing? (Chapter 6)
5. What is the third stage of healing?
   (Chapter 7)
6. How can we help in the healing journey? (Chapter 8)

As we walk through this journey of discovery, many feelings will surface. There will be times of sadness, joy, anger and love. It will be a more difficult journey for some because it is close to home. Looking at abuse is repulsive and heart-rending. We are assured, however, by having a Divine Companion who has walked the way before us. He knows the pain of wounds and is the El Rapha, the Lord that Heals. In Chapter 2, we will study the healing ministry of Jesus and learn principles that will guide our journey. "But to you who fear My name The Sun of Righteousness shall arise with healing in His wings. (Mal. 4:2) What a precious promise. We have nothing to fear as we take this journey together.

Chapter 2

The Healing Ministry of Jesus

*T*he first step in comprehending the road map for this healing journey is about Jesus, the Great Healer. In the work of ministering hope to the wounded heart, Jesus is our example. There are seven clear principles that comprise His healing ministry. Following these principles will enable us to extend the healing ministry of Christ to hurting hearts.

The acronym **H-E-A-L-I-N-G** will be used to present these important truths.

H = Healers Called
E = Entering Door
A = According to Faith
L = Lavish Love
I = Inclusive Restoration
N = Need Precedes
G = Gratitude and Glory

H = Healers Called

Healers are called and empowered by Jesus. He said, "Most assuredly, I say to you, he who believes in Me, the works that I do he will do also; and greater works than these he will do, because I go to My Father." (John. 14:12) The word, *assuredly*, means "made certain or guaranteed." We can know beyond a shadow of a doubt that if we believe in Jesus Christ, He will do great things through us – even greater than the things He did. It hardly seems possible, but Jesus himself says it; making it an iron-clad promise.

After the disciples spent time with Jesus, He called them to a healing ministry and sent them out two-by-two. He gave them power to "heal all kinds of sickness and all kinds of disease." (Matt. 10:1) When Jesus calls us to ministry, He gives the ability and strength to answer that call. Success in any healing ministry comes through faith in the promises of Christ.

Scriptures for Personal Study: Matt. 10, Matt. 13:58, Luke 9

E = Entering Door

The ministry of healing was a major part of Jesus' work on earth. Many Scripture references tell us that Jesus taught the people about the kingdom, preached the Good News and healed their diseases. Studying the words *teaching*, *preaching* and *healing* in the gospels provide some fascinating results. *Preaching* is mentioned the least – thirteen times. *Teaching* comes next at twenty verses and *healing* comes in first. *Healing* appears twenty-five times in a general sense such as, "For He healed many, so that as many as had afflictions pressed about Him to touch Him." (Mark 3:10) Not included in these general verses are stories of thirty-one individuals that Jesus healed. Healing is an important ministry; perhaps even more important than teaching or preaching, but certainly not less so.

As Jesus brought healing to the hurting and hopeless, their hearts were opened to the gospel. The ministry of healing to which God has called us is an entering door into the hearts of survivors. God will use us to bring healing, wholeness and good news to their hurting hearts.

Scriptures for Personal Study: Matt. 4:23-24, Matt. 9:35-36, Luke 6:17-19

A = According to Faith

In almost every story where Jesus heals someone, He speaks about the faith of the person being healed. Sometimes, as when the two blind men came for healing, Jesus began the healing by asking the person to declare their faith:

"Jesus said to them, 'Do you believe that I am able to do this?' They said, 'Yes, Lord.' Then He touched their eyes, saying, 'According to your faith let it be to you.' And their eyes were opened." (Matt. 9:28-30)

Other times Jesus said after their healing, "Your faith has healed you." (Luke 19:42) Healing takes place when someone believes that God can heal them. Faith is about hope and trust. It is saying, "God, I believe You can and will do this."

Faith is always a component of healing, but sometimes a helper's faith affects the healing. Jesus was healing and teaching in a very crowded home when four men tried to reach Him so their paralytic friend could be healed.

Unable get through the crowd of people, the men opened the roof over Jesus' head and let the paralytic man down on a stretcher in front of Him. Scripture says, "When He saw their faith," Jesus healed the man. (Mark 25) Clearly, intercessory as well as individual faith plays a part in healing.

This means that as we minister to survivors, our faith plays a part in their restoration. Jesus says to the survivor, "because I see the faith of those ministering hope to you, you are healed." What a precious blessing to be a pivotal part of God's amazing healing to survivors.

Scriptures for Personal Study: Matt. 8:5-10, Matt. 15:21-28, Mark 2:1-5, Mark 5:30-34, Luke 17:11-19, Luke 18:35-42

L = Lavish Love

Some of the most beautiful words in Scripture describe Jesus' love and compassion. "He saw a great multitude; and He was moved with compassion for them and healed their sick." (Matt. 14:14) *Com* means "with" and *passion* is "strong feeling." Compassion is indicated by coming alongside someone with deep love and sorrow for their pain. The Greek word for compassion means "being moved in one's bowels." It was thought the bowels were the seat of love and pity. Perhaps you've had the experience of watching a particularly pitiful picture of human suffering and your stomach literally aches. Our Lord's reaction to wounded people shows that compassion and healing are inseparable in the ministry of Jesus.

God calls us to be moved with compassion toward those who are hurting. Love is always a risk, which means we can and will hurt. It also means we share in the most precious work given to us as followers of Christ and our joy will be full.

Scriptures for personal study: Matt. 9:36, Matt. 15:32, Matt. 20:34, Mark 1:41, Mark 6:34, Luke 7:13

I = Inclusive Restoration

No person, place, time or condition was beyond the healing power of Jesus. He healed everyone who came to Him in faith: Jew and Gentile, male and female, rich and poor, young and old. He healed the outcasts, the lepers, the ritually unclean and the demon-possessed. From every walk of life, Jesus entered the space of the sick and suffering and offered healing.

Healing had no set place or time. It happened in the synagogue, the temple, the home, the roadside and the mountaintop. Jesus healed in the morning, at noon and during the night.

Jesus healed the whole person. He healed people spiritually, often before physical healing. "Your sins be forgiven you." (Matt. 9:2) Jesus healed physically – leprosy, blindness, paralysis, lameness and even death. Jesus healed people socially by restoring them to their families and communities. The hemorrhaging woman was a total outcast from society because of her condition. After healing her, He said, "Daughter, be of good cheer; your faith has made you well. Go in peace." (Luke 8:48) He restored her to her family and community. He healed cognitively by changing belief systems. Jesus, by word and action continually challenged beliefs. He changed despair to hope, indifference to love and fear to peace.

Scriptures for Personal Study: Matt. 12:10-13, Mark 5:1-15, Mark 7:24-30, Luke 8:43-48, John 18:10, John 4:46-54

N = Need Precedes

Jesus came to die so we could have the freedom of choice. God's system never includes forcing the will. We have the freedom to choose God's way or not. This principle permeated Jesus' healing ministry. Jesus asked the man at the pool of Bethesda, "Do you want to be made well?" (John 5:6) We must need and want healing in order to choose. Need has everything to do with freedom of choice. When we have a need, our hearts are open to choosing the remedy for that need. Need always precedes healing.

In some villages Jesus healed everyone. In Capernaum at the end of the Sabbath, "when the sun was setting, all those who had any that were sick with various diseases brought them to Him; and He laid His hands on every one of them and healed them." (Luke 4:40) But this didn't happen everywhere. Sometimes Jesus didn't heal people because they didn't feel their need and therefore choose healing:

"He could do no mighty work there, except that He laid His hands on a few sick people and healed them. And He marveled because of their unbelief." (Mark 6:5-6)

The people in Nazareth felt no need and were not open to His healing ministry. Our great need brings us to the feet of Jesus with open hearts to receive His healing.

Scriptures for Personal Study: Matt. 8:1-2, Mark 10:51, John 5:6

G = Gratitude and Glory

Jesus' entire healing ministry was to the glory of God. In referring to Lazarus, Jesus said in John 11:4, "This sickness is not unto death, but for the glory of God." Then again in verse 40, just before he calls Lazarus forth from the tomb, he says, "Did I not say to you that if you would believe you would see the glory of God?" Jesus never healed for His own glory even though he had a legitimate right to do so. It was always about God. Matthew 9:8 says that when the people saw the healing of the paralytic, "they marveled and glorified God."

Giving God glory is offering adoration, praise and thanksgiving. Gratitude and glory go hand-in-hand and to thank God is to give Him glory. There were ten lepers who came to Jesus to be healed and He told them to go to the priests to get a certificate of cure. As they were going, they were healed. "And one of them, when he saw that he was healed, returned, and with a loud voice glorified God and fell down on his face at His feet, giving Him thanks." (Luke 17:15) Our attitude of gratitude as we minister hope to hurting hearts is about God's glory. Everything we do and say is to God's glory. Nothing is about our glory; everything is about "walking and leaping and praising God!" (Acts 3:8)

Scriptures for Personal Study: Luke 13:10-13, John 9:23-25

Chapter 3

What causes wounds?

*U*nderstanding the definition and behaviors of abuse is crucial when ministering to survivors. Survivors tend to deny or minimize their abuse. To keep from becoming entangled in their denial system, we need to be clear about what abuse is. All the players are part of the denial system: the person abused, the abuser, anyone that could have or should have known about the abuse, and/or anyone who wanted the abuse kept secret.

Denial is often misunderstood. It is not, "I know what happened but I'm just pretending it didn't." Instead, it is "I will not let myself know that it happened." This defensive process occurs at a sub-conscious level and is a buffering response to abuse. In order for victims to survive and function in life, they often feel the need to deny what happened. Some have such a strong denial that they have no memory of the abuse until adulthood when some precipitating event blows the cover off their secret. More often, they remember that something happened, but remember only some portion of it. Even if they do remember, they minimize the impact of the event on their lives and separate the facts from their feelings. By putting things in separate compartments they dissociate fact from feeling - never allowing them to connect.

Although abuse has many faces, there is one overarching component. Almost all abuse is about power and control. The abuser controls the victim by any number of behaviors. Perpetrators manipulate their victims and make them objects to fulfill their own needs without regard to consequences for the victim. The control is often an immature reaction to life circumstances in which the abuser (usually in childhood) was put in a helpless situation. They have a strong need for mastery and control over the environment - human and physical. Many abusive behaviors can be traced to this helpless situation and their fear about a potential or actual loss of control.

Both victims and perpetrators are wounded, but because of our outrage regarding abuse, we can forget this. Research indicates about one-third to one-half of perpetrators were themselves victims.[12] Of course, not everyone who was abused becomes an abuser, and all abusers were not abused.

Ministering to the hurting heart means knowing what abuse is and never giving an excuse for it. Ultimately, abuse is sin. There is no excuse for sin. We may have compassion and understanding for the abuser, but it is never acceptable to abuse a child of God and we must stand firm on this truth.

The Metaphor of Wounds

Applying the metaphor of the physical wound to the wounds of abuse can help us gain an accurate picture of the different types of abuse.

One-time or Repetitive

A physical wound can be caused by a one-time event or by repetitive events. A single event can be a paper cut. A repetitive injury might be a blister rubbed raw by repeated friction. Similarly, the wounds of abuse can be a child fondled by a babysitter once, or repeated abuse like name calling and belittling over a period of years. While a physical wound caused by a single event can be minor or severe, repeated wounding generally causes deeper, longer lasting pain and takes longer to heal. The same is true with abuse; long-term repeated abuse takes longer to heal and usually affects the survivor to a greater degree overall.

Superficial or Deep

Physical wounding can be superficial or deep. Nicking your finger with a knife would be superficial, whereas fracturing a femur would be a deep wound. The resulting injuries would be quite different. The wounding of abuse can be superficial or deep as well. An incident with an older neighbor child coercing a child to play "doctor" a couple of times would be more superficial. It would require healing, but the healing time would be shorter and necessitate less energy. If someone were raped or beaten, this "deep wound" would entail a longer healing time and substantial support to heal. When the abuser is part of the trusted circle (family, church and friends), this wound becomes very deep. Healing from this wound requires extensive time, extra energy and significant support.

Systemic Factors

A physical wound can complicate the healing process if a person's body is impaired by decreased immune function, poor nutrition, or any number of other conditions. The effects will be more severe and take longer to heal. The same is true for wounds from abuse. When the family system is dysfunctional or when the abused has other problems like learning disabilities, low self-esteem, or physical impairments, then the emotional injury becomes more serious and healing more complicated.

Comparing a physical wound with wounds of abuse helps us to comprehend why some people have a more difficult time during the healing process than others. Age, severity, length of the abuse, level of support, length of time from the incident to when healing begins, whether the abuse was validated, relationship to the abuser and many more factors play a part in the length and difficulty of the healing process.

Many times we think we know what abuse is, but many of the beliefs we have are wrong. Here are some myths and facts about abuse:

MYTH: It's only abuse if it's violent.

Fact: Physical abuse is just one type of child abuse. Neglect and emotional abuse can be just as damaging, and since they are more subtle, others are less likely to intervene.

MYTH: Only bad people abuse their children.

Fact: While it's easy to say that only "bad people" abuse their children, it's not always so black and white. Not all abusers are intentionally harming their children. Many have been victims of abuse themselves, and don't know any other way to parent. Others may be struggling with mental health issues or a substance abuse problem.

MYTH: Child abuse doesn't happen in "good" families.

Fact: Child abuse doesn't only happen in poor families or bad neighborhoods. It crosses all racial, economic, and cultural lines. Sometimes, families who seem to have it all from the outside are hiding a different story behind closed doors.

MYTH: Most child abusers are strangers.

Fact: While abuse by strangers does happen, most abusers are family members or others close to the family.

MYTH: People lie about child abuse for attention and sympathy.

Fact: Research shows that it is very rare for a person to state they were abused when they were not; however, "false-negative reports" of abuse are common i.e. many adults state they were not abused as children when, indeed, they were. Police and court statistics also demonstrate that it is very rare for a person to fabricate a claim of child abuse.

23

When we look at specific abusive behaviors, we tend to think of some as much worse than others. While true to some degree, it's also important to remember, "When it comes to damage, there is no real difference between physical, sexual and emotional abuse. All that distinguishes one from the other is the abuser's choice of weapons."[13] As we've seen, all abuse is about power and control – treating people as objects.

Appendix I includes very detailed definitions of and indicators for abuse. I will include a shortened list here.[14]

Emotional Child Abuse

Remember the saying, "sticks and stones may break my bones but words will never hurt me?" Contrary to this old saying, emotional abuse can severely injure a child's emotional health and social development, leaving lifelong psychological scars. Examples of emotional child abuse include:

- Constant belittling, shaming, and humiliating a child
- Calling names and making negative comparisons to others
- Telling a child he or she is "no good," "worthless," "bad," or "a mistake"
- Frequent yelling, threatening, or bullying
- Ignoring or rejecting a child as punishment, giving him or her the silent treatment
- Limited physical contact with the child—no hugs, kisses, or other signs of affection
- Exposing the child to violence or the abuse of others, e.g. the abuse of a parent, a sibling, or even a pet

Child Neglect

Child neglect—a very common type of child abuse—is a pattern of failing to provide for a child's basic needs for food, clothing, hygiene, or supervision. Child neglect is not always easy to detect. Sometimes, a parent might become physically or mentally unable to care for a child. Other times, alcohol or drug abuse may seriously impair judgment and the ability to keep a child safe.

Older children might not show outward signs of neglect, and instead present a competent face to the outside world, or assume the role of the parent. But at the end of the day, neglected children are not getting their physical and emotional needs met.

Physical Child Abuse

Physical abuse involves physical harm or injury to the child. It may be the result of a deliberate attempt to hurt the child, but not always. It can also result from severe discipline, such as using a belt on a child, or physical punishment that is inappropriate to the child's age or physical condition.

Many physically abusive parents and caregivers insist that their actions are simply forms of discipline—ways to make children learn to behave. But there is a big difference between using physical punishment to discipline and physical abuse. The point of disciplining children is to teach them right from wrong, not to make them live in fear.

Physical Abuse vs. Discipline

In physical abuse, unlike physical forms of discipline, the following elements are present:

- Unpredictability. The child never knows what is going to set the parent off. There are no clear boundaries or rules. The child is constantly walking on eggshells, never sure what behavior will trigger a physical assault.
- Lashing out in anger. Physically abusive parents act out of anger and the desire to assert control, not the motivation to lovingly teach the child. The angrier the parent, the more intense the abuse.
- Using fear to control behavior. Parents who are physically abusive may believe their children need to fear them in order to behave, so they use physical abuse to "keep their child in line." However, what children are really learning is how to avoid being hit, not how to behave or grow as individuals.

Child Sexual Abuse

Child sexual abuse is an especially complicated form of abuse because of its layers of guilt and shame. It's important to recognize that sexual abuse doesn't always involve body contact. Exposing a child to sexual situations or material is sexually abusive, whether or not touching is involved.

While news stories of sexual predators are scary, what is even more frightening is a child is usually sexually abused by someone the child knows and should be able to trust—close relatives like fathers, brothers, uncles, cousins, etc. Contrary to what many believe, it's not only girls who are at risk. Boys and girls both may suffer from sexual abuse. In fact, sexual abuse of boys may be underreported due to shame and stigma.

Aside from the physical damage that sexual abuse can cause, the emotional component is intense and far-reaching. Sexually abused children are tormented by shame and guilt. They may feel they are responsible for the abuse or somehow brought it upon themselves. This can lead to self-loathing and sexual problems as they grow older—often either excessive promiscuity or an inability to have intimate relations.

The shame of sexual abuse makes it very difficult for children to come forward. They may worry that others won't believe them, or will be angry with them, or that it will split their family apart. Because of these difficulties, false accusations of sexual abuse are rare. So if a child confides in you, take him or her seriously. (See Appendix II for profile information on sexual perpetrators)

Chapter 4

What are the effects
of wounding?

*I*n Chapter 2, we saw the different types of wounds. Each wound will have an effect on the abused person and the variety of possible consequences is remarkable. These effects come from two sources. First, there is the damage of the wound itself. Abuse hurts and requires lots of love and attention for healing to occur. Second are the myriad coping behaviors a person uses to survive the wounding and avoid re-wounding. Going back to our metaphor of a physical wound will give us a clearer picture of how this happens.

Suppose you received a serious gash on your arm, you would go to the emergency room to receive care. The physician would stitch it up, apply medication and bandage it. During the next few weeks, you'd keep the wound clean, apply medication and generally follow the directions of the health care professional. You'd protect the wound from re-injury, keep your appointment to have the stitches removed and eventually the wound would heal, leaving only a scar to remind you of the wounding.

Suppose there were no one to help with this serious wound? Let's say someone was wounded and they covered it up, trying to live their life as though nothing had happened? The wound would likely get infected. It could get bumped and begin bleeding again. While this might sound absurd, let's follow the metaphor and we will see a vision of what can happen in the wounding of abuse.

So, here is this covered up, trying-to-be-ignored wound. What are some things the person might do to deal with this unattended wound?

29

- Avoid any contact where it might be bumped
- Take substances that would deaden the pain
- Focus on other things to avoid thinking about it (sleeping a lot, watching television, overeating, working overtime, etc.)
- Pay attention to someone else's pain

Well, you get the picture and you've probably already started to apply this to the wounds of abuse.

Children are amazingly creative beings. They don't have a lot of choices when it comes to abuse, but they choose and develop whatever coping strategies they can to survive their wounds. Many of these coping strategies are brought with them into adulthood. It is important to honor the way people have tried to survive the wounding of abuse. Some of these coping strategies are hurtful to themselves and others, but they did work at one point.

The following is a list of the coping strategies that children develop to deal with the unattended wounds of abuse.

1. Minimizing: means pretending that whatever happened wasn't really that bad.
2. Rationalizing: means inventing reasons to excuse the abuser. "Oh, he couldn't help it, he was drunk." "Four kids were just too much for her. No wonder she didn't take care of me."
3. Denying: means being able to say at a sub-conscious level that whatever is happening *isn't* or whatever happened *didn't*. "If I ignore it long enough, it will go away." It's often more comfortable for a child to deny reality than to face the fact that the adults around her wouldn't protect her, and in fact harmed her. Some may acknowledge the abuse, but deny the effects of the abuse.
4. Forgetting or Blocking: the mind's ability to block the abuse. This is one of the most common and effective ways that children deal with abuse. The mind has tremendous powers of repression. Many children are able to forget about the abuse, even as it is happening to them.
5. Lack of Integration: the feeling of being divided into more than one person. There is the little girl having the good childhood, but underneath there is the child who's prone to nightmares and sees people hiding in the corner of the room. In cases of extreme abuse, this kind of splitting can result in the development of multiple personalities.
6. Leaving your body: the ability to numb their bodies so they will not feel what is being done to them. They can actually leave their bodies (in their mind's imagination) and watch the abuse as if from a great distance.

7. Control: the capability to go to great lengths to keep their lives in order, especially if they grew up in a chaotic environment. They want to control their environment, themselves, and others. Perfectionism can be a part of this need for control.

8. Chaos: the aptitude for maintaining control by creating chaos. If their behavior is out of control, they force the people around them to drop what they're doing to respond to the latest crisis. Survivors are often good at both resolving and generating crises.

9. Spacing out: the capacity to zone out and be absent emotionally. This can be finding an object in the room and staring at it, or even walking into walls, doors or furniture - because they're not really present in their surroundings.

10. Being super-alert: proficiency at always being hyper-aware of the people around them, always anticipating their needs and moods. As a child, tuning into every nuance of their environment may have saved them from being abused.

11. Humor: a tough sense of humor, a bitter wit, or sense of cynicism, can get them through hard times. As long as they keep people laughing, they maintain a certain protective distance. And as long as they keep laughing, they don't have to cry.

12. Busyness: Staying busy can be a way to avoid feelings. Many survivors live their whole lives according to the lists they write first thing in the morning.

13. Escape: As a child or an adolescent, they may have made attempts to run away. If they were more passive, there was escape through sleep, books, and television. Sometimes children create fantasies - if they couldn't afford to believe the abuse was really happening, they could make believe something else was going on.

14. Physical complaints: Many victims fight memories and effects of their damage with physical responses to their inner pain, such as back and neck pain, and headaches.

15. Depression: It is easier and feels safer, many times, for survivors to turn hate toward themselves rather than feel the anger and hate towards the abuser.

16. Mental illness: Problems occur when the line between fantasy and reality blurs. For many survivors 'going crazy" makes a lot of sense. "I had to get sick to get away."

17. Self-mutilation: is one way survivors control their experience of pain. Instead of the abuser hurting them, they hurt themselves. Sometimes it is done because physical pain distracts from emotional pain.

18. Suicide attempts: sometimes a survivor feels like the only option left is to end one's life.
19. Eating difficulties: Anorexia, bulimia and compulsive overeating is another way of coping. Survivors may feel that being large will keep them from having to deal with sexual advances. Eating can be numbing or soothing to help ease the pain. Not eating can feel like asserting control instead of feeling powerless.
20. Lying: When children are told to never talk about the abuse or they don't want people to know what's really going on at home, they may become adept at lying. Survivors often become compulsive liars.
21. Stealing: is a totally absorbing activity. It enables them to forget everything for a brief moment, including the abuse. It is a way to create distraction or excitement, to re-create the feelings they had when they were first abused - guilt, terror, or the rush of adrenaline. Stealing is also a way of defying authority, an attempt to take back what was stolen, to even the score. It is also a cry for help.
22. Gambling: is a way to maintain the hope that life can magically change. It's a way to act out the longing that their luck could shift and there will be justice. If they win big, they will finally get their due. Gambling is also a thrill, a way to escape the difficulties and challenges of day-to-day life.
23. Workaholism: Survivors often feel an overwhelming need to achieve, to make up for the badness they can feel is hidden inside. Excelling at work is something they can control and that's given a lot of support in our high-achieving culture.
24. Avoiding intimacy: If they don't let anyone close to them, no one can hurt them. "I kept myself safe and alone."
25. Give me that old-time religion: Safety can be found by attaching themselves to a set of very rigid and tightly defined rules and beliefs. "I allowed no doubt. None. I did as I was told. I did not think."
26. Compulsively seeking or avoiding sex: If abuse was their sole means of getting physical contact when they were a child, they may continue to look for closeness only in sexual ways. They may become promiscuous or try to meet nonsexual needs through sex. Or they may go to great lengths to avoid sexuality. They may numb their body so that they don't respond sexually.
27. Drugs and alcohol: it numbs pain, and creates a sense of being alive or excitement for one who may feel "dead" inside.
28. Caretaker par excellence: Survivors can be extreme caretakers. A caretaker focuses on the needs and feelings of the other person instead of their own; they value being needed because they can't imagine being

wanted. They obsess on the other person's feelings and ignore their own.

Often there is a great deal of shame and self-blame that people experience when they have chosen some of these strategies. It is true that these behaviors are hurtful and therefore sinful. However, we need to help people to have compassion for themselves (and the child they once were) for creatively surviving some very painful and difficult wounding experiences. A big part of the work of healing is to let go of some of these strategies and replace them with healthy God-given ways to cope with life.

Before leaving this chapter on the effects of wounding, we'll explore three main feelings survivors experience: shame, contempt and powerlessness.

Ultimately, shame is the dread of being known. The fear is that if we are known, we will be seen as unlovable and worthless. Shame is a silent killer tucked away in the backpack of denial influencing every feeling and action. Everyone has lived with the bitter taste of shame, but those who are abused have a greatly intensified version of it.

Shame began in the Garden of Eden. When Adam and Eve disobeyed God's law, they felt exposed and disgraced. They hid and tried to cover themselves. This was and is a legitimate response to sin. The problem with abuse is that the abuser is the one who should experience the shame, but because they do not acknowledge or accept it, the survivor absorbs it like a sponge.

Even if the victim knows the fault or shame lies with the abuser, there is still shame. The most tender part of every one of us is the need to be loved, wanted and enjoyed. When that need is used and abused, we feel the shame of wanting love from someone who tosses us aside like a piece of dirty laundry.

Shame is also experienced as fear of exposure. Abusive family systems have various rules and one of them is "don't talk." Abuse is a secret and silence is required. If the survivor directly or indirectly lets the secret out; they feel responsible for the consequences to their abuser and family. If the survivor tells and the information goes unnoticed or is not believed, the abuser will make them pay for breaking the silence.

The second feeling is contempt, which is a type of condemnation toward the source of shame. Unfortunately, survivors see themselves as a source of shame and have great self-contempt. They berate themselves for the least mishap – lost keys, a mistake in writing or a misspoken word. In other words, a victim's head is a bad neighborhood to live in. This contempt can also be felt towards others as well; like the abuser and those who the abuser represents. For instance, if the abuser is a man, then all men can be seen as contemptible.

This contempt can come in all degrees. Very severe contempt includes serious physical self-destruction or mutilation. This can be as serious as suicide, or more subtle like eating in a self-destructive way. Severe contempt is about physical self-destruction. This contempt could also be directed at the abuser. The victim could become physically destructive to the abuser in an overt or more subtle way. Moderately severe contempt is exhibited by personal destructiveness and takes the form of violent fantasies toward oneself or dreams of revenge toward the abuser. Mildly severe contempt is the most common and especially for women can take the form of judgmental self-talk like trashing their body, hair, clothes, etc. Other-centered mildly severe contempt manifests itself as finding fault. Often this form of contempt is done quietly in one's mind. Being relationally uncomfortable is also a form of contempt as when someone is unable to receive a compliment. There can be a sense of unworthiness (self-contempt) or doubting the sincerity of the compliment (other-centered contempt).[15]

Contempt is also a coping behavior. It diminishes shame; "If I shame myself first, you have less power." Contempt deadens longing. Proverbs 12:2 says, "Hope deferred (lost) makes the heart sick." (NASB) The survivor has lost hope and is afraid to open their heart so contempt is an anesthesia for the heart's desires, i.e. "I didn't want it anyway." Contempt gives the abused an illusion of power. There is a feeling of having control over the other or oneself. Lastly, it takes the focus off the real problem (the need for healing) and focuses it on peripheral issues.

Powerlessness is a foundation feeling for all forms of abuse. The abuser strips the person of the ability to choose. The abused was powerless in three ways: 1) she was helpless to turn to her family to stop the abuse, 2) she had no power to stop the abuse herself, and 3) even after the abuse ended, she felt helpless to end the unremitting pain in her soul. The effects of powerlessness are despair (no amount of trying will end this nightmare) and deadness (the only way to survive the pain).

The unattended wound is covered with the bandage of deadness and as we've seen, the abused employ many behaviors to maintain that deadness. In the next chapter we'll begin to explore how to bring healing to the wounds of abuse.

Chapter 5

What is the first stage of healing?

*N*ow that we understand what causes a wound and the effect it has on survivors, we're ready to examine the stages of healing a person goes through. In this chapter, we will look at the beginning stage of healing.

Going back to our metaphor, suppose someone has had a wound for many years. They've kept it covered so no one knows it exists. Their coping skills have apparently worked and they may be functioning fairly well. So, what happens that brings the person to the point of caring for their wound?

Emergency Stage

The first stage of healing is called the emergency or crisis stage. The bandage isn't working at keeping the wound covered and forgotten. There are many things that can precipitate this stage.

- The survivor's child turns the same age they were when the abuse occurred.
- An experience occurs that mirrors the abuse experience.
- A person gets exhausted from all the energy it takes to keep things under wraps.
- Someone reveals the secret.
- The abuser dies or becomes ill.
- The coping strategies become more painful than keeping up the front.
- Their relationships are in crisis as a result of their coping strategies.

However it happens, the bandage starts to loosen and wear thin. The wound is crying to be seen and tended to. This is a frightening and overwhelming time for the survivor. Feelings of powerlessness during this stage mirror the abuse. Survivors have described their feelings as "being in the midst of a tornado," "like a volcano erupting," "everything in my life is falling apart" or "I think I'm going crazy." Survivors need to be reassured that these feelings are normal and they will pass.

The bandage that has been covering the festering wound for years is removed. Just as a person removes a bandage on a physical wound in various ways, the same is true for the wounds of abuse. Some people tear it off in one fell swoop. Others inch it off little by little. Some attempt to cover it up again and ignore it. Whether quickly or slowly, the result is the same; the wound is visible. They "look" at the ugly festering wound that needs care.

The emergency stage must be traversed to the other side. This is a normal part of the healing process. Some tools survivors need for riding this storm are: being gentle with themselves, creating a safe space, remembering to breathe and holding on to God's hand. A survivor's faith is tested and tried during this period. God's promises provide hope; they are not alone in the midst of the tempest. Psalm 31:7 says, "You have seen my troubles, and you care about the anguish of my soul." (NLT)

Choosing to Heal

Sometimes before this stage, but usually during this stage; the survivor is confronted with a real question: "Am I going to choose to heal from the wounds of abuse?" The decision to heal is a radical, God-honoring, life-affirming choice. They may have been running from this wound for years, even decades. Deciding to stop running, remove the bandage, look at the wound and actively seek healing takes a great deal of courage. This is a very difficult, but vital, choice. Feelings of powerlessness have been part of their experience, often their whole lives. First, during the abuse control was used and they felt helpless. Next, they felt compelled to hide the wound for years. Then, during the emergency stage, they feel forced to deal with an avalanche of feelings. Freedom of choice is the only antidote to the feelings of powerlessness. Christ died for the power of choice. Survivors can choose whether they will heal or not. Healing is difficult and painful. A reality that helps many survivors is this, "You will have pain; the question is whether you will choose the pain of healing or the pain of a festering wound?" Another powerful question for them is, "Would you be willing to give as much commitment to healing as you did to surviving and covering?" Choosing healing may be hard, but is so worth it in the end.

Remembering and Believing

Remembering the abuse is part of the emergency stage. Earlier I listed some events that can precipitate this. These events touch the wound and memories come roaring to the surface. Even if the abuse were part of the survivor's conscious awareness, much of it has been minimized and denied. Overwhelming feelings now surface with the known facts. New memories rush in like a flood. We often think of memories as things we "see" from the past like a snapshot or a film. However, memories reside in any or all of the five senses. Abuse causes memories to become fragmented or disassociated so they surface in bits and pieces. A person may "see" bloody sheets or a door knob turning. They may "hear" a hurtful name or a crying child. They may "smell" alcohol or sweat. They may "feel" terror or pain in part of their body. They may "taste" blood or semen. We think of memories as residing in our brain or thoughts. Scientists have discovered that memory also resides in the body. One client developed bruises on her legs in the shape of a hand where she had been repeatedly hit as a child. It seems that the body remembers what the mind wants to forget.

Memories are a "gift" that assist the survivor; helping them to believe the truth of the abuse. Believing is an important part of the healing process. John 8:32 says, "Ye shall know the truth and the truth shall set you free." While this is certainly speaking of theological truth, I believe it also applies to the truth of abuse. I've seen clients have repeated memories and dreams. When they accepted that the abuse did happen, these diminished or stopped altogether. It seems memories serve a function of bringing the secret to the surface. When that truth is acknowledged, there is less power in the memory or dream.

One example is a client I'll call Sally. She had dreams of a "shadow man" turning the doorknob of her room and starting to enter. She would wake up in a panic. This dream occurred frequently over a period of years. She had a conversation with her sister about it. Her sister said, "Don't you remember Dad coming into our bedroom at night to molest us?" After a period of struggling with that truth, she accepted it. Once she believed it, the dream of the "shadow man" never returned.

When memories are so vivid the survivor feels the abusive experience again, these are called flashbacks. When the survivor experiences a flashback, they feel immersed in the past abusive experience either as a participant or an observer. Flashbacks are a symptom of Post-Traumatic Stress Disorder (PTSD) and can be very dramatic and frightening. Any traumatic experience such as abuse, accidents, natural disasters, war, etc. can result in a diagnosis of PTSD.

Healing is a process that takes a great deal of time and energy. Think of recovering from the flu or a fractured femur. You need to conserve your physical strength, get extra sleep, drink lots of fluids, eat well, and take appropriate medications. Emotionally you withdraw from the larger world and surround yourself with caring people where you can be yourself. Spiritually you seek God's presence and care. "He shall cover you with His feathers, and under His wings you shall take refuge." (Ps. 91:4) Some people try to recover and change nothing about the pace of their lives. This does not work because recovery is too exhausting.

Telling the Truth

The old bandage is off and the wound is visible. What has been hidden for years is now known to the survivor and usually to those close to them. Breaking the silence with truth-telling is a powerful part of healing, but it is not easy. Survivors have become experts at being silent. Abusers repeatedly threaten abused children with the death of a family member, a pet or themselves if they tell anyone about the abuse. The child may have gathered courage and told someone, but often they were called a liar or even blamed for the abuse. Frequently the courageous act of telling increased the abuse.

Once a survivor decides to tell, the question is, "whom do they tell?" Telling has pitfalls and mines to be navigated. It is important to choose the person(s) carefully. Trusting someone to see their festering wound and hear about how it got there is very vulnerable. Safety and trust are key elements in open sharing. In the early stages of recovery it is almost always unwise for them to tell the abuser, anyone who disbelieved them in the past or anyone invested in protecting the abuser. They may consider telling a loving spouse, a trusted friend and/or a counselor. Telling another survivor can be very healing.

To a survivor, breaking their silence feels like a leap in the dark; the consequences cannot be predicted. Speaking about the abuse brings considerable shame in its wake. However, telling is the only way through the shame and taking that leap is transformative. Over and over I've seen people gather courage, face their fears and tell their story. The results are stunning. They no longer feel alone. Freedom and relief take the place of bondage and burden.

Ministering during the Emergency Stage

Helping someone deal with memories is part of the ministry to hurting hearts. First, it is important to "honor" the memory. Saying, "maybe you're just imagining it" is feeding into their already active denial system. As we've seen, the body (through memory) remembers what the mind wants to forget so memories should be believed. Any little word of doubt can send the person back into their denial cave. In all my years of counseling, I've never experienced someone make up abuse. More damage is done by disbelieving a victim than we can ever imagine. I'd rather believe them and be wrong perhaps .001% of the time.

Second, listen to them with nonjudgmental compassion. Talking about the memories and abuse is helpful when someone listens well. Listening is one of the most important skills you can have when ministering to survivors. How well you listen has a major impact on the quality of your relationship with them. Most people are not good listeners. Research finds that we remember only 25-50% of what we hear. This means in general, people listen to only half of a conversation. Clearly, as we minister to hurting hearts we want to listen well. This includes active and passive listening. (See Appendix III) Perhaps one of the major values of counseling is someone listening with compassion. Survivors often grow up in a home where no one listens to them. Since parents are the first authority figures they know, this can put a wedge between God and them. In my work with survivors I've found they often need an experience of someone "in the flesh" listening to them. Then they are better able to accept God as a Gracious Listener.

Third, if they are having a flashback, the most helpful thing you can do is to support them in becoming grounded in the present. This is done through the five senses. They can feel their body against the chair or hold a piece of ice. Speak to them and have them answer you or turn on some loud praise music. Have them smell some strong peppermint or take a bite of a lemon. Have them take an inventory of everything around them by describing the colors or counting the pieces of furniture. You want to do anything that will bring them back into the "here and now." (See Appendix IV for more about PTSD and flashbacks.)

The fourth way to minister to hurting hearts during this stage is to reduce their burdens by giving them extra help. They often feel overwhelmed and frazzled. This is especially true of mothers with young children. Giving them a break to complete some of their healing work or just rest is truly a ministry of healing. If you ask, "How can I help?" the person might be at a loss to answer. It's more useful to ask, "Would it help if I... (specific action)," or "I would like to... (specific action), is that OK?"

Lastly, here are some miscellaneous ways you can support survivors. Write them a note to tell them you're praying for them. Tell them what you're praying. You can pray specific Scriptures for individuals such as Romans 15:13, "[I pray that] the God of hope [will] fill you with all joy and peace as you trust in Him, so that you may overflow with hope by the power of the Holy Spirit." (NIV)

Survivors need some light times as well. Make celebration a regular part of your relationship with them. Celebrate their victories and milestones - large and small - with a note, with lunch together, a single flower or some other small symbolic gift.

Especially during this phase, realize the power of your presence. Just being there is encouraging to them. When you're with them, you're telling them they're important. The Apostle Paul closed his letter to the church at Colossae promising to send his friend Tychius "that he may encourage your hearts." (Col. 4:8)

Chapter 6

What is the second stage of healing?

*I*n Chapter 5, we examined the Emergency Stage of the healing process. In this chapter, we look at what comes next once the bandage is removed and the wound is visible. Carrying through our metaphor of the physical wound, the first thing that would happen after the bandage was removed is an assessment. We'd ask questions like: What kind of wound is it? What caused it? What kind of treatment does it need?

Debriding False Beliefs

An unattended physical wound would be in dreadful condition. There would be infection and dead sloughing skin. Generally, the first treatment would be debridement which is described as "removal of dead, damaged, or infected tissue to improve the healing potential of the remaining healthy tissue."[16] Applying this to the emotional wound, we might think of damaged or false beliefs that survivors develop because of the abuse. Our beliefs come from our experiences. Children who grow up in a dangerous home believe the world is a dangerous place. So, if I believe the world is dangerous, I would be fearful. Feelings are the result of our beliefs. I might have different ways to deal with that fear, i.e. bravado, hyper-vigilance, or over-control. A major work of healing for the survivor is identifying and disposing of damaging dead beliefs. We'll examine three of the major damaging beliefs that poison the survivor.

All abuse is ultimately spiritual abuse, so the first major deadly belief centers on their relationship with God. False beliefs about God are numerous. Fear and sometimes anger are the feelings that result from these beliefs. Survivors may believe God is impotent or untrustworthy to care for or hear them. "If He didn't stop the abuse, why should I trust Him now?" "He's just not as powerful as people think." They may believe He is a vengeful God who would "zap" them if they do something wrong. "I deserve to be punished." God might seem manipulative like their abuser. "If I don't do what He says, He'll make me pay." Capriciousness is another belief about God. "I always feel like something bad is around the corner." "I never know when the other shoe will drop." They may believe that God has abandoned them. "If He really cared, He would have protected me." If the abuse was perpetrated by a religious person, they can believe the church is abusive as well. If the survivor tried to tell someone at church and the person turned a blind eye to the abuse, the church might also be seen as uncaring.

The second major deadly belief is the abuse was their fault or they should have stopped it. Guilt and shame are the feelings that result from this belief. Often children were told by their abusers they were responsible for what was happening. One abuser begged the child to make him stop the abuse while continuing to perpetrate the abuse and thus showing to the childish mind that they were to blame. It is difficult for children to believe that someone they love (especially a parent) is defective or hurtful. So, if something wrong or bad is happening, they see it as their fault. Survivors say, "I was such a bad kid, they had to discipline me like that", or "but I liked the attention so I must have wanted it to happen", or "I was older and I should have known better." Abuse is never the fault of a child. Even if a fourteen or fifteen-year-old girl were to dress provocatively and "throw" herself at her father, it is his duty to resist. It is unfair to expect children to protect themselves. It is always the responsibility of adults to treat children with respect. Jesus speaks some strong words about this: "But if you cause one of these little ones who trusts in me to fall into sin, it would be better for you to have a large millstone tied around your neck and be drowned in the depths of the sea." (Matt. 18:6 NLT)

Thirdly, survivors believe they are unworthy, bad and defective. "I'm bad for being the cause of my family's problems." "I hate myself." This belief results in shame and fear. Shame is different than guilt. Guilt generally stems from what we do that we see as wrong, but shame is about who we are. Survivors' sense of shame permeates their life and relationships. They fear others validating how worthless they believe they are. As a means of control, the abuser may have told them they were no good, worthless or stupid, thereby making them slaves to any words or actions of approval from the abuser. During her recovery, one survivor was asked to look in the mirror and say one thing she liked about herself. Dissolving in a pool of tears, she couldn't think of anything.

Especially for sexual abuse survivors, this feeling of worthlessness and shame is attached to their bodies. They see their body as dirty and shameful. If there was physical pleasure attached to the abuse, this feeling and belief only intensifies. You can't stop your stomach from digesting a sandwich. It's the physiology of the body. In just the same way, you can't stop your body from responding to sexual stimulation even if unwanted or violent. Sexual response does not mean the survivor was responsible in any way.

Ministering to Hurting Hearts during the Debride-ment Stage

Confronting damaging false beliefs is the major work of this stage of healing. . A simple model for understanding why it's so important to change these beliefs is as follows:

Experiences = Thoughts or Beliefs = Behaviors and Feelings

This is what happens. The experiences cannot be changed; they are a reality. The behaviors and feelings are a direct result of the thoughts and beliefs. The only hope then for real transformation is changing the thoughts and beliefs. What we have just discussed about beliefs in counseling circles is called cognitive therapy. Whether or not you're a therapist, there is much you can do to help survivors confront and change these damaging false beliefs. Looking at some biblical concepts should make it clear why this is such a major part of healing from abuse.

Scripture affirms, "For as he thinks in his heart, so is he." (Prov. 23:7) It would be difficult for someone who believes they are worthless or bad to have any other feeling than shame. Scripture again affirms this principle. "Whatever a man sows that will he also reap." (Gal. 6:7) If we sow damaging beliefs, we will reap negative feelings and until the beliefs are changed, survivors will be trapped in harmful destructive feelings. The only way out of this "bad neighborhood" that is the survivor's head is through changing thoughts and beliefs. The best way to make that change is through the Word of God. "We all . . . by beholding . . . are being transformed . . ." (2 Cor. 3:18)

Refuting these deadly beliefs can only be done through Christ and His Word. We can minister to survivors by sharing God's truths. Survivors need to hear three kinds of truths from scripture to refute the damaging beliefs resulting from abuse. Understanding God's real character is the first truth. Second is His great compassion for the oppressed and his rage at the oppressor. Third is how much He values and loves us, His children. Here are some healing texts from God's Word that expresses these truths. I know you will be able to think of many more as you pray and work with survivors.

- Jeremiah 31:3 - Yes, I have loved you with an everlasting love; Therefore with lovingkindness I have drawn you.
- Isaiah 43:1 - But now, this is what the Lord says - He who created you, He who formed you; 'Fear not, for I have redeemed you; I have summoned you by name; you are mine.
- Romans 8:35, 37-39 - Who shall separate us from the love of Christ? Shall tribulation, or distress, or persecution, or famine, or nakedness, or peril, or sword? (*we might add abuse here*) Yet in all these things we are more than conquerors through Him who loved us. For I am persuaded that neither death nor life, nor angels nor principalities nor powers, nor things present nor things to come, nor height nor depth, nor any other created thing, shall be able to separate us from the love of God which is in Christ Jesus our Lord.
- Paraphrase of 1 Corinthians 13:4-7 substituting God for the word love since God is love. (1 John 4:8) "God is patient; God is kind; God is not envious or boastful or arrogant or rude. God does not insist on His own way; He is not irritable or resentful; He does not rejoice in wrongdoing, but rejoices in the truth. He bears all things, believes all things, hopes all things, endures all things." (NRSV)

God's Word is indeed the best source for changing thoughts and beliefs which will in turn change behaviors and feelings. Survivors desperately need to see God's love expressed towards them. As we help them confront their false beliefs, we must work carefully and respectfully. They must know our belief in them and our hope in their healing.

Believing that God abandoned them because he didn't stop the abuse is a major issue for survivors. As we minister to them around this issue, we must never give an excuse for the sin of abuse. It is always inexcusable. Also, when a survivor uses the words, "Why did this happen?" or "Why did God allow this?" often, it is best to be present and listen. They may not be asking for an answer, they may need someone to hear their pain.

If they really are asking for feedback on this issue (and it's OK to ask them if they would like some), then there are some things we can share. For instance, abuse is only one of many, many cruelties occurring every day in our sin cursed world. Sickness, accidents, crimes, wars, famines, earthquakes, storms and the like are common occurrences. God created a perfect world and placed Adam and Eve in this paradise. He gave Adam dominion over it. Eve chose to trust Satan's lies rather than God's truth. Adam followed her in her obedience to Satan and thereby gave his God-given dominion over the world to Satan. Satan became the present god of this world system that operates on greed, power and lust and he ushered in sin, disease and death, "and the whole world lies under the sway of the wicked one." (1John 5:19) Jesus said that in the world, we would have trouble. (John 16:33) Scripture has many promises, but these promises are about God being with us in our pain; not necessarily shielding us from it. For example, "Even when I walk through the darkest valley, I will not be afraid, for you are close beside me." (Ps. 23:4 NLT)

The last truth, and the most important, is that Jesus died for the sovereignty of the human will. God allows people to choose. We wish people wouldn't choose to abuse others, but they do and they will ultimately bear the consequences of that choice. The tragedy is that innocent people get hurt in the process. Survivors had no power to stop the choices their abuser made. The good news is that they can choose to seek healing from the Great Healer and Lover of all.

Study the Word and God will show you many powerful texts to combat false beliefs as you minister to hurting hearts. Here is a wonderful promise when someone is feeling hopeless and overwhelmed found in Romans 4:18. The survivor can put their name in the blank and personalize it. "When everything was hopeless, ___(survivor's name)_____ believed anyway, deciding to live not on the basis of what she saw she couldn't do but on what God said He would do." (Message)

Drainage and Cleansing

After debridement, drainage and cleansing are the next step necessary in healing a wound. Following our metaphor, this stage of healing is about grief and mourning. Grieving is always a part of the healing process. The survivor needs to understand what was lost, taken or destroyed. These are some losses related to abuse:

- Loss of feelings (when painful feelings are buried, joyful loving feelings are also deadened)
- Loss of innocence
- Loss of protection and safety
- Loss of time and money while they heal from the abuse
- If the abuse was a family member, loss of intimacy and love with that person
- Loss of energy from years of hiding the wound
- Loss of the picture they may have had of a happy family

There are many other losses related to abuse; grief is very personal and unique to each person.

There were two major findings on grief and loss according to research done by William Worden and the Harvard Bereavement Study.[17] The first finding states that when someone has had a death or loss, that person must grieve. When mourning is absent, delayed or masked, there are consequences related to physical and emotional stress. Buried grief poisons and limits the capacity for joy and spontaneity for life. The second finding is that there are four tasks of mourning. These tasks are relevant to grieving survivors.

Accepting the loss is the first task. Survivors need to realize that they have lost many things related to the abuse. When they accept the reality of the abuse and the accompanying losses; denial, rationalizing and minimizing fade away. They begin to see how much they have been affected by what happened. Then they can move to the second task which is feeling the pain of the loss. Survivors could not do this work as a child. The feelings of agony, terror and fury without support would have been too devastating to bear. However, suppressed feelings are not resolved feelings. Expression of pain, sadness and anger allows release and letting go. Grief has its own rhythms and people can move fairly quickly from one feeling to another during this stage. Saying, "OK, now I'm going to grieve and feel" doesn't seem to work. Instead, there needs to be a space for grieving which allows (but does not force) it to surface. This work of grief is "draining and cleansing the wound."

Survivors shut down feelings related to abuse and often describe themselves as feeling dead inside. These feelings were blocked at the time the abuse began so when the feelings begin to surface they can be very strong and primitive. One survivor working on the second task of grieving described it this way, "When I started feeling sadness, I felt like a little girl." Another person said, "I thought that if I started to cry, I'd cry for the rest of my life." BIG emotions are a central part of the grieving process.

Not only can feelings be overwhelmingly powerful, they can be confusing. If the abuse was perpetrated by a loved one, the survivor can feel intense love and strong hate toward them. Having two very strong seemingly opposing feelings is difficult to acknowledge, feel and express.

Tasks three and four are accomplished during the next stages of healing. The third task is becoming accustomed to the changes related to the loss. This can include things like changes in the family structure or the relationship with the abuser especially if they are parents or other close family members. The fourth task is withdrawing energy from the loss/abuse and reinvesting it into other people or things.

Ministry during the Draining and Cleansing Stage of Healing

Feelings of grief can be very intense. People in grief don't need words, they need touch and presence. Sitting with someone as they grieve, holding their hand and listening to their pain; this is the important work of ministry. Many helpers are uncomfortable with pain and they try to "fix" it. I remember when my grown son experienced a great loss. I wanted to pick him up and kiss his "booboo" and make it all better. Of course I couldn't do that, but even if I could have, that would have been the wrong thing to do. People who have a death or loss must, for their health's sake, grieve. We do them a disservice if we try to stop it. Part of the work of preparation to minister to hurting hearts is to deal with our own grief and pain so we can be there for them.

Anger is a particularly difficult feeling for a lot of people and especially Christians. The Bible is instructive regarding the expression of anger. Many survivors find the book of Psalms very helpful. David seems to have been an expert on grief. David was real and his feelings were authentic and raw. Over and over he ranted and raved about injustice and abuse, and then he came back to this: "God, I don't understand it, but I trust in You."

Ephesians 4:26 says, "Be angry, and do not sin." Anger is an emotion which is neither right nor wrong; neither good nor bad. It is what we do with anger that causes sin. Survivors need to be angry about the abuse. God is angry about abuse. However, in the expression of their anger, they may not hurt themselves or someone else. A helpful way to express the anger is to write a letter without censor, but don't send it. They can read it to someone (or not) and then burn it or shred it. I've seen survivors throw stones over a cliff, rip up a phone book, beat a pillow, or lie on a bed and have a temper tantrum. I've seen survivors be angry with the abuser, the people who knew about it and didn't stop it, the people who should have known about it and even God.

People who minister hope need to be accepting of people's anger. When someone is deeply hurt, anger is a natural human response. Jesus was angry when people hurt other people. One survivor said, "When I'm angry, it's because I know I'm worth being angry about." Some survivors are afraid if they get angry, God will abandon them. We need to be able to assure them God is bigger than anger and that he holds them in the hollow of His hand while they rage. Sometimes people fear they will stay stuck in their anger. What I have seen in my work with survivors is that if they keep expressing, they will move through these feelings to the other side. In the process, they will become more alive to express the whole range of feelings open to us as children of God. When people continue to suppress angry feelings, they live in a chronic state of anger (minimal or considerable). It's often just below the surface. They may not even be aware of it, but others, especially their children are aware. It's like living with a volcano; you're never sure when it's going to erupt, but you know it's there seething under the surface.

God desires us to be authentic and bring everything including our rage to Him. Being dishonest with God is useless, he knows what we feel already. God says, "Come, just as you are and tell me about it." God's promise is that He reaches "from on high and takes hold of me; He draws me out of deep waters. He rescues me. He brings me out into a spacious place. He rescues me because He delights in me." (2 Samuel 22:17, 18, & 20 NLT, adapted)

Chapter 7

Stage Three

*F*ollowing the metaphor of the wound, we've explored the uncovering, assessment, debridement, draining and cleansing of the wound. The next step would be the application of curative treatment. The wound would need some kind of medicine to promote healing. Of all people, survivors desperately need healing salve applied to their wounds. After suffering and struggling with the pain of abuse for years, it is a relief to feel the soothing balm. There is a beautiful promise about healing in James. I've added some words to adapt it for survivors. "Are you hurting? Pray. Do you feel great? Sing. Are you sick (*wounded*)? Call the church leaders (*fellow survivors and support people*) together to pray and anoint you with oil (*healing salve*) in the name of the Master. Believing-prayer will heal you, and Jesus will put you on your feet. And if you've sinned, you'll be forgiven—healed inside and out." (James 5:13-15 Message)

Healing salve comes in several ways: self-care, boundaries, forgiveness and spiritual nourishment.

Healing Salve of Self-Care

Survivors are notorious for not taking care of themselves. Either they feel unworthy of self-care or they avoid their needs by being totally focused on others. Learning and practicing self-care is important because healing takes a lot of energy and stamina. When we are physically sick (like healing from a surgical wound), we need to take extra care of ourselves like getting enough sleep, drinking fluids, eating well, etc. This need for physical care is also present when healing from the wounds of abuse.

Survivors were not cared for very well as children. Part of the work of healing and restoration is learning how to give themselves physical, emotional, cognitive and spiritual care. There is a concept of the "inner child" which is part of many recovery models. The basic premise is that the child we once were is still a part of our experience. Indeed, every experience and every age we've ever been is part of who we are today – for good or ill. For the survivor, learning to care for that hurt, wounded, vulnerable, scared part of them is applying healing salve.

We tend to treat our inner child the way we were treated. For the survivor, this may mean they neglect their physical need for rest, food or medical care. One survivor said, "I was so out of touch with my body, I'd end up really sick and wouldn't have noticed the symptoms until they were severe, and even then I kept pushing myself."

Survivors also treat themselves emotionally the way they were treated. Everyone does something called self-talk. This is an internal ongoing monologue usually operating just below our conscious awareness. We speak about 100-150 words per minute, but our self-talk moves at 600-800 words per minute. We tend to speak to ourselves in ways that we've been spoken to. Survivors that were yelled at, called names and told they were stupid, for instance, speak to themselves in the same way. In working with clients, I've asked them to become aware of their self-talk. They come back horrified at the things they say to themselves. Imagine what it would be like for them. What if someone was following you around all day saying those negative hurtful things to you? Maintaining a happy joyous spirit would be very difficult. Part of the work of healing is changing that continual flow of unkind upsetting messages.

Ministering with the Healing Salve of Self-Care

As we help apply the healing salve of self-care to survivors, we must also practice self-care. This is important for two reasons. First, how can you teach self-care if you are not practicing it? Our example is a big part of our ministry. Second, and even more important, the work of ministry is difficult. Giving of yourself in this way requires physical, emotional, cognitive and spiritual strength. If you're not taking care of yourself, you will be burned out. People talk about Jesus as our example. They mention how he stayed up all night and worked all day. Remember that Jesus ministry at this pace was for three and a half years. The disciples of Jesus needed to learn how to work and how to rest (self-care). Today we need to listen to the command of Christ, "Come aside by yourselves to a deserted place and rest a while." (Mark 6:31) I especially like Jesus' words in The Message paraphrase of Matthew 11:29-30, "Come to me. Get away with me and you'll recover your life. I'll show you how to take a real rest. Walk with me and work with me — watch how I do it. Learn the unforced rhythms of grace. I won't lay anything heavy or ill-fitting on you. Keep company with me and you'll learn to live freely and lightly." (Messge)

Appendix V includes a list of things that are part of self-care. This will be helpful in your work with survivors, but I suggest you take a personal inventory and see how you're doing in these areas of self-care. Jesus said, "Freely you have received, freely give." (Matt. 10:8) Jesus was speaking to His disciples who had spent times of nourishment with Him. If we don't receive (nourishment), we can't give (nourishment).

Actually, survivors have attempted to care for themselves. All the strategies used by them to cope with the abuse discussed in Chapter Four are attempts at self-care. They can be affirmed in their attempts and gently led to more wholesome ways of nurturing their body, mind and spirit.

Part of the work for survivors is learning they are valuable in God's eyes and He affirms their need for self-care. Often survivors think self-care is selfish. The truth is God gives us our lives and tells us to be good stewards. This means we take care of ourselves for God's glory. We are God's temple and the place we connect with the Holy Spirit. A dilapidated, broken-down, abandoned temple wouldn't be a very good place to worship God. "Do you not know that your body is the temple of the Holy Spirit who is in you, whom you have from God, and you are not your own? For you were bought at a price; therefore glorify God in your body and in your spirit, which are God's." (1 Cor. 6:22) We have been bought with a costly price which makes us precious. The word precious means "of great value; not to be wasted or treated carelessly."

Paul writes some powerful words to the Thessalonians. I have paraphrased them in a different verse order and changed them into the first person. "I am learning to appreciate and give dignity to my body, not abusing it. God, you haven't invited me into a disorderly, unkempt life but into something holy and beautiful — as beautiful on the inside as the outside. I choose to keep doing what will please You, not in a dogged religious plod, but in a living, spirited dance." (1 Thess. 5, 7 & 1 Message)

Healing Salve of Boundaries

Boundaries are a big part of self-care. They include our inner life: feelings, wants, needs, thoughts, beliefs, intuitions, decisions, beliefs, choices, etc. Physical boundaries involve touching, physical closeness, sexual behavior, privacy (mail, journals, doors, private spaces, nudity), clothes, gifts, food, property, money, time and energy. All of these are individual to each person.

Drs. Cloud and Townsend in their seminal book on boundaries talk about three principles related to boundaries.[18] The first concept is "me and not me."

Being created in God's image means I have stewardship over my life. What does that mean? What am I responsible for? We need to know what is included when God says, "Here is your life, tend and keep it." Proverbs 14:10 says, "Each heart knows its own bitterness, and no one else can fully share its joy." (NLT) Knowing what is me and not me gives me clear information about what I am and am not responsible for. For instance, we do not own other people's feelings and they do not own ours. We are not asked to change or control others, although a lot of time and energy is spent in trying to do so.

The second concept flows from the first one. We are responsible to others and for ourselves. Galatians 6 has what at first appears to be two opposing commands. Verse 2 says, "Bear one another's burdens, and so fulfill the law of Christ." On the other hand, verse 5 says, "For each one shall bear his own load." If we understand the Greek meaning of the words burden and load, these apparently contradictory instructions will become clear. Burden is defined as an abundance of weight. This would be like a large boulder so heavy there is no way someone could carry it alone. When someone is ill (recovering from the wounds of abuse) or has experienced a major loss, the burden is too heavy to shoulder alone. Others come alongside to help bear the burden. The term load could be defined as a knapsack. You are responsible for carrying your own knapsack for the day's duties. Perhaps you've met people who try to make others responsible for their knapsack or conversely people who are unwilling to help someone carry a heavy boulder. What a relief to know I am responsible for my own knapsack and not someone else's. When we carry someone's knapsack, we do them a huge disservice! We steal from them! On the other hand, what a joy to know I can be responsible to (not for) someone with a heavy burden to bear.

The third concept is about "good in and bad out." Proverbs 4:23 says, "Above all else, guard your heart, for everything you do flows from it." (NIV) Guarding something means you keep the good in. If you were guarding sheep, you wouldn't let them wander from your property. Not only would you keep the good in, you'd invite the good in from the outside. You'd let in the delivery truck bringing grain to feed the sheep. Guarding also means keeping something bad out. You would keep predators away from the sheep. So, good in and bad out. Abuse turns this upside down. Survivors close themselves off to the good and open themselves up to the bad because that's what they experienced growing up. Reversing this process is part of the healing salve of self-care. Let the good in and keep the bad out!

According to Nina Brown, there are four main types of psychological boundaries.[19]

- Soft - A person with soft boundaries merges with other people's boundaries and is easily manipulated.
- Spongy - A person with spongy boundaries is a combination of having soft and rigid boundaries. They are unsure of what to let in and what to keep out.
- Rigid - A person with rigid boundaries is closed off so nobody can get close to him/her either physically or emotionally. This is often the case if someone has been physically, emotionally, psychologically or sexually abused.
- Flexible - This is the ideal. The person decides what to let in and what to keep out, is resistant to manipulation and is difficult to exploit.

A big part of healthy boundaries is the ability to say yes and no. Jesus, in talking about oaths during His Sermon on the Mount said, "Let your 'Yes' be 'Yes,' and your 'No,' 'No.'" (Matt. 5:37) He was saying, "Just tell the truth." Being able to say "No" is part of defining our boundaries. Toddlers say "NO" a lot and loudly. This helps them define their wants and needs and is a part of healthy development. Shaming children for saying, "No" stunts their ability to set boundaries. Affirming children for saying, "No" and allowing children to make the choices they can will go a long way toward advancing healthy self-care. Let them say, "No, I don't want to wear that shirt" or "No, I don't like broccoli."

"No" is such a little word, only two letters, but so very powerful. Many Christians feel guilty when they say "No"; so they say "Yes" and don't mean it. One client said, "I could never say 'No' growing up. If I tried I was severely punished. So I learned to say 'Yes' which basically meant I was lying a lot of the time." Truly, if you don't have the ability to say "No," then your "Yes" is not really a "Yes." Practicing "No" is a valuable part of the healing salve of boundaries.

Ministering with the Healing Salve of Boundaries

In ministering to survivors, Jesus is our example in the area of boundaries. Jesus did not force people. Force is against the nature of God. Freedom of choice is a highly prized treasure in the bank of heaven; Jesus died for it. It's true God tells us about the consequences of our choices, but the choice is ours, none-the-less. In the story of Mary and Martha, Martha clearly wanted Mary to come and help her. Perhaps Martha had taken on more than she could do, which would be a boundary issue. Mary was saying "No" to spending time in the kitchen. Jesus was present and she wanted to drink in every word. Martha appealed to Jesus to "make" her sister help her. Calling her name twice for emphasis, He told Martha that Mary had chosen to sit at his feet and He wouldn't take that away from her. As you minister to survivors who have a hard time saying "No," share with them the stories showing how Jesus respected people's boundaries and choices even if they were harmful.

Working with survivors can be frustrating at times. We can have an agenda for them and they may reject it. We must work on knowing what our responsibility is versus theirs. You may be the safest person in their life to say "No" to and they may need to practice saying it a lot. On the other hand, you need to say "No" as well. Taking care of your boundaries is a wonderful example for survivors.

There is a spiritual lesson we can share with survivors related to the concept of "bad out." When we open up and communicate our pain to God and others, we let the bad out and we can be healed. Letting the "good in" means opening the heart to God's spiritual gifts. "Every good gift and every perfect gift is from above, and comes down from the Father of lights, with whom there is no variation or shadow of turning." (James 1:17) Not only does He give good gifts, but He is safe and trustworthy; He never changes. His love and care for us is constant and reliable. Consider ministering to a survivor by hunting the scriptures together for treasure. Find all the treasures that are "good in."

Healing Salve of Forgiveness

The topic of forgiveness is challenging for survivors. It's hard because there are many misunderstandings about forgiveness. Lewis Smedes, in his book *Forgive or Forget*, explores the process.[20] Four tasks must be completed to forgive. The first two are "hurting and hating." This means we have to feel the pain of grief and rage in order to be able to forgive. The third step is healing. This comes after the hurt and hate is fully acknowledged. We begin to see the person who hurt us with different eyes and we begin to let go of the resentment and rage. The last stage is reconciliation or coming together. This stage may or may not happen. If the abuser does not acknowledge the wounds they inflicted, then reconciliation puts the survivor or people close to them (often their children) at risk for re-wounding. It is appropriate that abusers suffer the consequences of their behavior. Forgiveness is one thing, nullifying consequences is another.

We will look at this process through the eyes of a survivor. "For many years I knew intellectually that my father had sexually abused me and I thought I had forgiven him. As I began the work of recovery, I realized I hadn't allowed myself to really acknowledge how much I was hurt by his behavior. For many months I cried and raged about the hurt and pain of the abuse. I continued to pray and ask God to do His work in me. Gradually I began to see how sick and wounded my father was. I began to see his wounded child. I also saw he refused to acknowledge his behavior. This concerned me because I had children of my own. How could I know that they were safe? I struggled with this. One day as I was praying, I became aware that I was no longer raging about my father, I no longer wanted him to hurt the way he had hurt me. I felt a sense of calm. I knew that I had forgiven him. However, because of his lack of ownership about his abuse and my concern for the safety of my children, I had a very minimal relationship with him."

In this story, we see the four tasks of forgiveness: hurting, hating, healing and reconciliation (or not). Here are more truths about forgiveness:

- Forced forgiveness is not forgiveness.
- Unless someone experiences the feelings connected to the hurt, they have not forgiven; it's called pseudo-forgiveness and many Christians are guilty of it.
- Forgiveness is a process that usually takes time, it is rarely instantaneous.
- Forgiveness is a gift from God.
- Forgiveness never means that what the person did was acceptable.
- Forgiveness is a gift the survivor gives themselves; it isn't done for the perpetrator.
- There can still be feelings of anger or hurt after the forgiveness, but the resentment or holding it against the person is gone.
- Forgetting the hurt is not a necessary part of forgiveness.
- Forgiveness is the natural resolution of the grief process.
- Forgiveness in no way requires that you trust the one you forgive. It doesn't mean the relationship must be restored.
- Forgiveness does not depend on the other person's action or inaction – "I'll forgive you, if you_____."

It is not necessary for the perpetrator to ask for forgiveness in order for the survivor to heal. Sometimes the perpetrator lives at a distance or has died. However, if the abuser does repent and ask for forgiveness, the survivor generally has an easier work of letting go of resentment. 2 Chronicles 7:14 is a good model for abusers who seek forgiveness from their victims. "If My people who are called by My name will humble themselves, and pray and seek My face, and turn from their wicked ways, then I will hear from heaven, and will forgive their sin and heal their land." This would include several steps.[21]

1. Acknowledge the sin specifically
2. Confess the wrong doing
3. Repent - a total change is required

4. Ask for forgiveness - the person who has sinned needs to ask God and the person that has been harmed for forgiveness
5. Offer restitution in one way or another.

Ultimately, forgiveness has nothing to do with absolving the abuser. It has everything to do with releasing oneself from the burden of being a victim and being transformed from victim to survivor to thriver. "When you release the wrongdoer from the wrong, you cut a malignant tumor out of your inner life. You set a prisoner free, but you discover that the real prisoner was yourself."[22]

Ministering with the Healing Salve of Forgiveness

When working with survivors around forgiveness, great tact and tenderness is needed. Forgiveness is a touchy subject for survivors. The more they look at and deal with the wound, the more real the abuse becomes. This honest appraisal brings up feelings of hurt and anger. As helpers, we need to remember that forgiveness is a process. It takes time. Our job is to provide a safe space for the survivor to move through the process.

As helpers, we need to examine our lives to see if there is a need for forgiveness. The word *resentment* comes from *re* meaning again and *sentiment* or feeling. It is feeling something over and over again. It's those situations in life that we rehearse over and over. They re-surface when we least expect them; the old feelings are still present and we are experiencing them again. One way to work on old angers is to make a resentment list. Write down people, events, institutions, etc. that you have some "charge" about. This is your unfinished business. Take the list and pray about it. Ask God to give you forgiveness. Journaling about the items on your list can help you get clear about exactly why you have feelings of resentment about that issue. Write an honest letter to the person that you don't plan to send. (You can always write a letter you plan to send after you've done your work on the issue.) As you work through the process of forgiveness, you will be better able to minister hope to hurting hearts.

Healing Salve of Spiritual Nourishment

The most significant healing salve is spiritual nourishment. All healing comes from God. Our bodies were created by Him with the ability to heal. When a wound happens, a myriad of body systems are activated and millions of cells assemble to do their work. The healing from wounds of abuse also comes from God and His healing salve.

Scripture uses several words for a medicinal ointment which is applied to a wound. Balm is one of those words. The term "balm in Gilead" comes from a region of ancient Palestine known for its balm taken from a small evergreen tree with aromatic leaves. Perhaps you've heard the beautiful song, *Balm in Gilead*, a much loved Black-American spiritual.

There is a balm in Gilead
To make the wounded whole;
There is a balm in Gilead
To heal the sin-sick soul.

Survivors need their wounds made whole and Jesus, the Chief Physician, is ready to dispense the balm of Gilead to the sin-sick soul. The balm of Gilead is bestowed through relationship with the Healer. That relationship is strengthened through spiritual practices. For survivors there are three simple, but important, spiritual practices to consider: prayer, scripture and spiritual writing. In setting aside a personal devotional time each day to include these practices, survivors will hear the words of mercy flowing from the lips of Jesus and those words will indeed be the balm of Gilead to their souls.

Personal devotional time (PDT) is a regular daily time set aside to nurture relationship with the Great Healer. "When" doesn't matter, some people are owls and some are chickens. What does matter is consistency. Setting aside a specific place for PDT is very beneficial. Some people chose a place in nature, a special room at home or even a church. One survivor said, "I have a place in my bedroom, a white wicker chair, where I meet God. Whenever I sit down there, my mind, body and soul seem to quiet down. I'm ready to open my heart and talk and listen." That special place can include things that direct your attention to God. Besides a Bible and a journal, there can be music, a picture, a candle, a sculpture, etc. One survivor remembers having a treasure box as a child that she kept in various secret places. It contained trinkets with memories and meaning attached. She decided to make a spiritual treasure box. She says, "I have a lot of things that have spiritual significance to me, like a feather that was a little gift from God, a rock taken from the shores of Lake Michigan during an especially meaningful time of connection with Jesus and a long red ribbon from the last session of a retreat where the song, 'The Joy of the Lord is My Strength,' gave me courage to do the work of healing." The PDT space should be unique to the survivor and their needs.

Prayer is often misunderstood and buried under habits and traditions that diminish its power and intimacy. Prayer is above all about relationship. It's about opening your heart. Intimate friendships involve honesty. Survivors can pour out their sadness, anger, joy and pain to God with complete abandon.

Survivors are afraid of their BIG feelings and often fear God's reaction to them. The truth is that God is bigger than any human feeling and "God is the rock of my refuge." (Ps. 94:22) Temper tantrums are allowed – no lightning strike will be forthcoming.

While studying scripture during PDT, survivors need to make the words real and personal to them. Here are some suggestions:

- Take a word, look it up in a concordance and read all the verses in the Bible that include that word. Some wonderful words to look up are love, hope, joy, salvation and healing.
- Go through the gospels and stop at the stories of Jesus' healings. Survivors can put themselves into the story. Jesus gave wonderful parables, symbolic stories, to reflect upon. These stories go deep into the heart and nourish the soul.
- Get a book that has Bible promises in it and look them up. Survivors can personalize them, write them down and journal about what they mean to them.

Spiritual journaling is a written record of personal reactions on spiritual matters. It provides a cathartic dumping ground for thoughts, feelings and ideas. A spiritual journal is a place to be honest. Regular journaling might include prayers, meaningful quotations, confession of sin, personal struggles, daily events of spiritual significance, insights, praise and thanksgiving, God's leading, joys, hurts and pain.

Ministering with the Healing Salve of Spiritual Care

Ministering to the hurting heart takes boundless wisdom from above. The only way spiritual helpers can acquire that wisdom is through spending time with Jesus and the Word. Make it your first priority each day to pray for the survivors God has put on your heart. There is a beautiful promise in Isaiah about God saving our children from giants and slavery. I believe we can apply this to our spiritual children as well. "Can plunder be retrieved from a giant; prisoners of war gotten back from a tyrant? But God says, 'Even if a giant grips the plunder and a tyrant holds my people prisoner, I'm the one who's on your side, defending your cause, rescuing your children.'" (Isa. 49:24-25 Message) What a precious promise; God is on our side saving our spiritual children. Faithfulness in our PDT is the core of our work with survivors.

After the last supper, just a few hours before His arrest, Jesus talks to his disciples and then prays for them. "I do not pray that You should take them out of the world, but that You should keep them from the evil one." (John 17:15) We too can pray this powerful promise for our spiritual survivor children. Make it personal by putting their name in the verse. "Lord, keep ___(survivor's name)___ from the evil one."

In ministering the salve of healing, we can help them remove some blocks they may have towards God. Survivors who were abused by their fathers and/or males may need to think of God in different terms. Appendix VII has a biblical list of names for God. We know that God is bigger than any gender box. Helping survivors choose a term with less "charge" will dismantle the wall that survivors may have toward God because of the abuse.

Chapter 8

How can we help in the healing journey?

W e've learned about Jesus, our example, in healing ministry. We've examined abuse, its effects and the stages of healing. In this chapter, we'll explore the role of helpers and how we can best support the healing journey of survivors.

Called to Minister

The story of Peter's mother-in-law is instructive for us as we minister to hurting hearts. Imagine how Matthew tells the story. Jesus is in Capernaum and is looking forward to spending time with Peter and his family. Entering the house, He sees Mother lying on a bed very sick with a fever. Jesus approaches her with great compassion. He touches her hand and immediately the fever is gone. Her skin returns to a normal hue and she opens her eyes to the tender face of Jesus bending over her. Full of energy, she joyfully rises and ministers to Jesus' needs.

The Greek word, *diakoneo*, means "to minister." The word "deacon" is derived from this word and is used in all three gospels to describe what Mother does after she is healed. Here is a gracious grateful woman. Jesus healed her from disease and possible death and she joyfully cares for his needs. This is the only narrative of Jesus' healings where the person responds to healing by immediately giving service.

Her story is our story. Jesus approaches us with great compassion. He touches us. We open our eyes to see His tender face bending over us. We are healed and full of energy and we joyfully rise and minister to Jesus' needs.

What a precious privilege to be called to serve our Healer, Jesus Christ. When we care for his beloved, we are caring for Him. "I tell you the truth, when you did it to one of the least of these my brothers and sisters; you were doing it to me!" (Matt. 25:40 NLT)

Daily we are to receive from Heaven the healing balm of God's grace and to allow that balm to flow through us to soothe the wounds of suffering survivors. As we do this we are proclaiming the gospel. The very essence of the gospel is restoration and Jesus is the great Restorer. What a high calling to be laborers together with Christ in caring for hurting hearts.

This work God has called us to do is not easy. You will at times wonder, "What was I thinking?" But know this; God has called you, not because you're smarter or more capable than someone else. We are weak vessels, easily broken. He called you because He loves you and wants to partner with you in a sacred endeavor. He will be with you every step of the way. 2 Corinthians 4:7-9 & 16 gives an amazing picture of ministry. "We now have this light shining in our hearts, but we ourselves are like fragile clay jars containing this great treasure. This makes it clear that our great power is from God, not from ourselves. We are pressed on every side by troubles, but we are not crushed. We are perplexed, but not driven to despair. We are hunted down, but never abandoned by God. We get knocked down, but we are not destroyed. That is why we never give up. Though our bodies are dying, our spirits are being renewed every day." (NLT)

God often calls people to minister who have been wounded themselves. Scars are the lasting record of having been wounded and every scar has a story to tell. Bill survived the Vietnam War and is eager to show his wound and tell the story about a buddy who saved him from death. Sarah survived thyroid cancer and shows the scar at the base of her neck as a testament to what she endured. Scars speak of the pain of wounding and the joy of healing. Every survivor has a story full of suffering and grace. God calls survivors to share their experiences as an inspiration for others on the healing journey.

Asymmetrical Relationships vs. Wounded Healer

Any relationship or social situation in which one person has authority over another is asymmetrical because the balance of power is more or less one-sided. This type of relationship is seen with doctors and patients; teachers and students. For instance, when someone has more knowledge than another or the ability to give consequences to the other person; there is imbalance of power. Often as helpers we can see ourselves as knowing more than the one we're helping. We may think we have it all together. We see ourselves as "one-up" which puts the survivor "one-down." Most of us wouldn't say this is how we feel or think, but we can feel this way and the message can even be conveyed unconsciously. We see ourselves as the mighty helper who must rescue the poor survivor. This is entirely against heaven's methods.

We need to come alongside survivors as fellow sufferers on the road of life. We are all wounded in one way or another. Jesus calls us to minister to hurting hearts because He has ministered to our hurting heart. The power of love was in all Christ's healing and we are instruments of His because we have received of that love. When we come to minister hope, we don't come with embarrassment hiding our wounds. We come sharing our wounds and the healing we've received. As followers of Jesus we allow our wounds to bring healing to others, just as Jesus' wounds bring us healing. "By His stripes we are healed." (Isa. 53:5)

Jesus told a story about two men who went to the temple to pray - the Pharisee and the tax collector. When we come to survivors as if we had it all together, we are like the Pharisee who prayed, "God, I thank You that I am not like other men . . . even this tax collector." (Luke 18:10) The truth is we are very much like others; we need God's grace and healing every day. Our daily prayer needs to be the prayer of the tax collector, "God, be merciful to me a sinner!" Jesus went on to say, "everyone who exalts himself will be humbled, and he who humbles himself will be exalted." (Luke 18:13-14) Humbly, we all meet on our knees at the foot of the cross.

Sacred Space

There is a precious promise given by Jesus. He says, "For where two or three are gathered together in My name, I am there in the midst of them." (Matt. 18:20) When we are ministering to a hurting heart in the name of Jesus, He is right there with us. That means the space we're in is sacred. Jesus, the Great healer is very near; an observer and participant in our ministry. God with us, Immanuel!

Sacred space happens when people feel safe. Safety is something many survivors never experienced. Supporting them to have that experience is essential to the healing process. The first way to create safety is through confidentiality. As helpers, we must keep their confidences. Never, unless their safety is at stake, should one detail of what they have told us escape our lips without their permission. This includes not telling details of their story. It's a small Christian world and telling details of a story could identify the person even if we don't tell their name. This also means we don't bring a prayer request to the church with any specific details unless we have their permission. We need to have a conversation with them reiterating our commitment to confidentiality. Then we must faithfully keep that commitment, no matter what.

A second way to create safety is to have boundaries around our sacred space. If the survivor is working on sharing emotionally sensitive things, decide on a time frame and choose a private space without interruptions. Having a time and space container helps create safety.

Musician Tom Kendzia composed a beautiful song based on Matthew 18:20. The words of the chorus are, "Where two or three are gathered in my name love will be found, life will abound. By name we are called, from water we are sent: to become the eyes and hands of Christ." When we spend time with hurting hearts—ministering, listening, laughing and praying—we indeed become the eyes and hands of Christ. What an exquisite privilege. Being with a person in pain, offering our presence to someone feeling hopeless, sharing times of doubt and uncertainty—these experiences can bring us profound joy. When two people have opened their heart to each other and God, there is a sweet sacred space surrounding them. Have you ever noticed someone's face after they have shared their pain and cried from their heart? There is an inviting vulnerability; their inner spirit, refreshed by Jesus, shines out in their beautiful face.

Circle of Support

When we examine God's methods in the world, we see that He uses people to minister to other people. God works with groups. The Godhead is three persons. God called the people of Israel. Jesus called disciples. The early church met in homes and shared their lives. Lone Rangers just don't make it in the Christian life. There are two ways we can apply God's principles expressed in the circle of support.

First, the survivor needs more than just you to support them. Being the end all and be all for them is damaging to them and pushes us towards burn-out. Helping a survivor create a circle of support is part of our ministry to them. Applying the healing salve takes more than just one person. Eventually, many people need to be part of the circle. Some possibilities are:

- Other survivors
- Spouse
- Friends
- Pastors
- Other church members/leaders
- Therapists (counselors, massage therapists, etc.)
- Physicians, nurses, etc.
- Groups (church groups, therapy groups, survivors' groups, 12-Step programs, etc.)

- Nutritionist
- Exercise coach

The options are many and varied. Survivors tend to pull back and isolate. This is what many did as children to survive. Empowering them step-by-step to include others in their lives is a valuable part of healing.

The second application of God's circle of support principle relates to us. As we minister to hurting hearts, we need other people to support us. Jesus sent out his disciples two by two. The apostle Paul and other early church leaders worked in pairs. God's plan is for people to support each other. We need that support for several reasons. First, often when two or more people work together, they both don't get discouraged at the same time. One person can express hope and minister comfort to the other.

Secondly, we need accountability. Working with a circle of support helps us see things we may not see. Are you getting caught up in the drama of the survivor? Are you spending too many hours helping and neglecting your own self-care? It's often hard to see these things ourselves; we need a circle of support to point them out. Good therapists have something called *supervision*. They meet with another professional who is a trained supervisor and talk about their clients. The feedback they receive helps them to see if they are missing something with a client or letting their own issues intrude on the work being done. We need "soul supervision" to make sure we are staying balanced and Christ-centered. Thirdly, there is power in group prayer. Abuse is satanic and we need much prayer as we help survivors combat the evil one. And fourth, we need someone in the flesh who loves us well. We need to "let our hair down" and laugh and be silly. We need to be nourished as we give to others.

Think carefully about who you will include in your circle of support. Pray about it and ask God to guide you. Once you are clear about whom to include, go to them and specifically ask them if they will be part of your circle of support. Don't leave it to chance or assume they know. Make it a commitment between you. Decide on a time when you will meet on a weekly or bi-weekly basis. Continually seek God's wisdom for your circle of support.

Hope

As you minister hope to the hurting heart, one of your major roles is to be the "holder of hope." Miriam ministered to the hurting hearts of the children of Israel. Even though we know nothing from scripture about Miriam between the saving of Moses and the Exodus, we can make a reasonable guess of some things about her during that time. Scripture tells us that Miriam was a prophetess and musician. These gifts didn't just appear at age 90 after crossing the Red Sea at the time of the Exodus. She was likely exercising these gifts throughout her life in ministry to God's people. Miriam, along with many others, had the hope of freedom from bondage. That hope centered on Moses as being the one to lead the people out of bondage, especially because of his miraculous rescue as a baby. Imagine Miriam's great disappointment when he killed a man and ran away.

Even in her disappointment I think Miriam had great hope in the Lord's promise of delivery from oppression. There must have been songs with deep meaning that kept hope alive among God's people. I believe that Miriam was a significant leader in this process; a "holder of hope." Music and movement have such wonderful power. Perhaps these songs and rituals were very similar to the songs of slaves in our own country some 150 years ago locked in oppressive slavery. Think of their songs: *Soon I Will Be Done with the Troubles of the World*, *Swing Low Sweet Chariot*, or *Amazing Grace*. These songs brought the hope of freedom and a vision of a better time and place. They bathed the people in peace and healing.

Survivors are often overwhelmed with the healing process. They cannot see to the other end of the dark tunnel of pain and rage. They often ask, "How much longer?" When the way seems very dark, it is often our hope that carries them along until they can hope again. It is our privilege to shine the light of God's love into their darkness and say, "Hope a little longer, there is light at the end of the tunnel, soon you will be free from the bondage of the past." We might say with the Psalmist, "O Israel (*survivor puts their name*), hope in the Lord; for with the Lord there is unfailing love. His redemption overflows." (Ps. 130:7 NLT) We are the "holder of hope" for the wounded heart.

Hope means to have confidence and trust that what is desired will be fulfilled. Hope and trust travel together in the journey of life. Our strength to minister comes from our hope in and trust of the promises of God. "Because of his glory and excellence, he has given us great and precious promises." (1 Pet. 1:4 NLT)

God promises His Spirit. "I pray that God, the source of hope, will fill you completely with joy and peace because you trust in him. Then you will overflow with confident hope through the power of the Holy Spirit." (Rom. 15:13 NLT) We need the mighty energies of the Holy Spirit with quickening, curative, transforming power to bring healing to the sin-bruised soul.

God promises to complete the work He starts. "Being confident of this very thing, that He who has begun a good work in you will complete it until the day of Jesus Christ." (Phil. 1:6) That promise gives us the hope He will complete the work in us and in the survivors we are ministering to.

God promises that he will comfort and use us. "All praise to God, the Father of our Lord Jesus Christ. God is our merciful Father and the source of all comfort. He comforts us in all our troubles so that we can comfort others. When they are troubled, we will be able to give them the same comfort God has given us." (2 Cor. 1:3-4 NLT) We can apply the comforting Balm in Gilead to the wounds of survivors because it has been applied to our wounds.

We are to carry the message of hope and mercy. No longer are survivors to be wrapped in the darkness of midnight without hope. The gloom is to disappear in the bright beams of the Sun of Righteousness.

This is my prayer for you and your ministry: "I pray that your hearts will be flooded with light so that you can understand the confident hope He has given to those He called—His holy people who are His rich and glorious inheritance. I also pray that you will understand the incredible greatness of God's power for us who believe him." (Eph. 1: 18-19 NLT)

Appendix I

Comprehensive Definitions of Abuse

*T*he Child Abuse Prevention and Treatment Act[23] has these definitions: Neglect is any recent act or failure to act on the part of a parent or caretaker, which results in death, serious physical or emotional harm, sexual abuse or exploitation, or an act or failure to act which presents an imminent risk of serious harm.

- Physical neglect – Includes abandonment or inadequate supervision, and failure to provide for safety or physical needs. Includes failure to thrive, malnutrition, unsanitary conditions, or injuries from lack of supervision.
- Educational neglect – Includes not enrolling child in school, or allowing child to engage in chronic truancy.
- Emotional neglect - Includes withholding of affection or attention, failure to provide psychological care, ignoring the child's emotional needs.
- Medical neglect – Includes delay or denial of dental or health care, or withholding medical care due to religious beliefs. Some states will not prosecute due to withholding of health care due to religious beliefs but court orders are occasionally obtained to save a child's life.

Physical abuse is the most obvious form of abuse. It is an act that results in physical injury to a child.

- Punching, beating, kicking, biting, burning, breaking bones, hair pulling and shaking a baby are examples of physical abuse.

Physical Abuse Indicators:

- Recurrent injuries with unexplained, guarded, implausible, or inconsistent explanations
- Uncommon locations for injury (underarms, neck, back, genitals, stomach, thighs)
- Lacerations, welts, oddly shaped or patterned bruises or lacerations (from an object)
- Burns (cigarette, immersion)
- Broken bones and intracranial trauma
- Hair loss
- Wearing long sleeve clothing out of season (hesitation on showing certain body parts)
- Acts out aggression on others
- Fear, withdrawal, depression
- Nightmares, insomnia

Sexual abuse is any misuse of a child for sexual pleasure or gratification. It is the involvement of children in sexual activities that they do not fully comprehend, that they are unable to give informed consent to and/or that violates societal taboos.

- Non-touching sexual abuse - Indecent exposure or exhibitionism, exposure to pornographic material or any sexual act, including masturbation.
- Touching sexual abuse – Fondling, making a child touch an adult's or another child's sexual organs, penetration of a child's vagina or anus by an adult or an object, and any other sexual act with a child.
- Sexual exploitation - Engaging a child for the purposes of prostitution or using a child to film or photograph pornographically.

Sexual Abuse Indicators:

- Compulsive masturbation, teaching others to masturbate
- Excessive curiosity about sex or seductiveness
- Sexual acting out with peers, others
- Bruises or bleeding in external genitalia or stained, torn, bloody underclothing
- Frequent, unexplained sore throats, yeast or urinary infections

- Complains of pain or itching in genitalia
- Difficulty in sitting or walking
- Excessive bathing
- Withdrawn or aggressive
- Sexually transmitted diseases
- Pregnancy, especially in early adolescence
- Substance abuse
- Overly compulsive behavior
- Fears and phobias
- Running away
- Sleep problems
- Depression
- Somatic symptoms (stomach aches, headaches, etc.)

Emotional abuse is a pattern of behavior that can seriously interfere with a child's positive development, psyche and self-concept. Emotional abuse is hard to identify due to no physical evidence.

- Rejection and Ignoring – Telling a child in a variety of ways that he or she is unwanted, having a lack of attachment, showing no interest, not initiating or returning affection, and/or not listening to the child. Not validating feelings. Breaking promises. Cutting the child off while he or she is speaking. Pretending to hear concerns, but then disregarding them.
- Shame and Humiliation –Telling a child he or she is stupid, etc. or evoking criticism when performance is not perfect. Judging what the child does as wrong, inferior, or worthless. Using reproaches such as "You should be ashamed of yourself," or "Stop crying or I'll give you something to cry about." Pride is also a feeling that is often met with shameful condemnations, such as "Who do you think you are, Mr. Big Shot?"
- Terrorizing – Accusing, blaming, insulting, criticizing, punishing and threatening with abandonment, physical harm, or death. Sabotaging success by making unreasonable demands or labeling the person as a loser. Taking advantage of the person's weakness or manipulating. Slandering.
- Isolating – Not allowing the child to engage with peers or activities, keeping a child in a room or small area, and not exposing the child to stimulation. Withholding information.

- Corrupting - Engaging children to witness or participate in criminal acts such as stealing, drug dealing etc. Telling lies to avoid justifying actions or ideas.

Emotional Abuse Indicators

- Hiding his or her eyes; lowering his or her gaze
- Annoyance, defensiveness, angry acts
- Exaggeration, confusion or denial
- Poor self-esteem
- Angry acts
- Withdrawal, insecurity, depression, suicide attempts
- Alcohol, drug abuse, or eating disorders
- Difficulty in relationships
- Sleep disorders/nightmares
- Nervous disorders or somatic symptoms
- Spiritual Abuse is the misuse of a spiritual position of power, leadership, or influence.
- Mind control or thought reform.
- Psychological, sexual, and/or physical abuse or assault
- Withholding needed medical care in lieu of prayer.
- Using religious texts for justifications for abuse.

Satanic or Sadistic Ritual Abuse (SRA) is an organized, secret, often multi-generational group who engage in mutilation, ritual killing, cannibalism, drinking of blood, systematic torture to produce robot-like, programmed, children, etc. Common Characteristics of Abusive Groups:

- Authoritarian – The group claims to have been established by God and leaders in this system claim the right to command their followers. Followers may be told that God will bless their submission even if the leadership is wrong.
- Image Conscious - History, character flaws, etc., are misrepresented or denied to validate the revered image of the group. Irrationally high standards are placed upon followers and their failure to live up to these standards is a constant reminder of the follower's inferiority to his or her leaders.
- Suppresses Criticism – Questions or open discussions about issues are not allowed. The group or religion is promoted as favored by God and a person who questions becomes the problem rather than the issue he or

she raised. Questioning anything is considered a challenge to authority and doubting God.

Spiritual/Ritual Abuse Indicators

- Child believes he or she is evil or causes others to be evil
- Mistrust of others outside the group
- Strong fear of God
- Overly obedient or perfectionistic
- Strong feelings of shame or guilt
- Programmed statements or behaviors
- Sleep problems or nightmares

The following is taken from the U.S. Department of Justice Office on Violence against Women:[24]

We define domestic violence as a pattern of abusive behavior in any relationship that is used by one partner to gain or maintain power and control over another intimate partner. Domestic violence can be physical, sexual, emotional, economic, or psychological actions or threats of actions that influence another person. This includes any behaviors that intimidate, manipulate, humiliate, isolate, frighten, terrorize, coerce, threaten, blame, hurt, injure, or wound someone.

- Physical Abuse: Hitting, slapping, shoving, grabbing, pinching, biting, hair pulling, etc. are types of physical abuse. This type of abuse also includes denying a partner medical care or forcing alcohol and/or drug use upon him or her.
- Sexual Abuse: Coercing or attempting to coerce any sexual contact or behavior without consent. Sexual abuse includes, but is certainly not limited to, marital rape, attacks on sexual parts of the body, forcing sex after physical violence has occurred, or treating one in a sexually demeaning manner.
- Emotional Abuse: Undermining an individual's sense of self-worth and/or self-esteem is abusive. This may include, but is not limited to constant criticism, diminishing one's abilities, name-calling, or damaging one's relationship with his or her children.
- Economic Abuse: Is defined as making or attempting to make an individual financially dependent by maintaining total control over financial resources, withholding one's access to money, or forbidding one's attendance at school or employment.

- Psychological Abuse: Elements of psychological abuse include - but are not limited to - causing fear by intimidation; threatening physical harm to self, partner, children, or partner's family or friends; destruction of pets and property; and forcing isolation from family, friends, or school and/or work.

Domestic violence can happen to anyone regardless of race, age, sexual orientation, religion, gender, socioeconomic backgrounds and education levels. Domestic violence can happen to intimate partners who are married, living together, or dating.

Domestic violence not only affects those who are abused, but also has a substantial effect on family members, friends, co-workers, other witnesses, and the community at large. Children, who grow up witnessing domestic violence, are among those seriously affected by this crime. Frequent exposure to violence in the home not only predisposes children to numerous social and physical problems, but also teaches them that violence is a normal way of life - therefore, increasing their risk of becoming society's next generation of victims and abusers. (See Appendix VII for more information)

Appendix II

Profiles of Sexual Abusers

*A*pproximately 400,000 convicted pedophiles currently reside in the United States, according to Department of Justice estimates.[25]

Types of Abusers:[26]

1. General or Situational Child Molesters– does not prefer children, but offend under certain conditions.
   o Regressed – Typically has relationships with adults, but a stressor causes them to seek children as a substitute.
      ▪ Eighty to ninety percent are male.
      ▪ At least one-third were abused themselves.
      ▪ They rarely molest family members.
      ▪ The 10% who do molest family members do so repeatedly and more severely.
      ▪ Step parents are ten times more likely to molest.
      ▪ They are rarely caught.
      ▪ In 50% of cases there is an alcohol connection.
   o Morally Indiscriminate – All-around sexual deviant, who may commit other sexual offenses unrelated to children.
   o Naive/Inadequate – Often mentally disabled in some way, finds children less threatening.

2. Preferential – has true sexual interest in children. These are what we call pedophiles. The term "pedophilia" refers to persistent feelings of attraction in an adult or older adolescent toward prepubescent children,

whether the attraction is acted upon or not. A person with this attraction is called a "pedophile"

- o Mysoped – Sadistic and violent, target strangers more often than acquaintances.
- o Fixated – Little or no activity with own age, described as an "over-grown child." The following are research findings by Emory University psychiatrist Dr. Gene Abel which have also been validated by other researchers.[49]
  - Most pedophiles molest boys.
  - If they do molest girls, it is 8-10 year olds
  - Men who molested boys had an astonishing average of 150 victims each.
  - Male offenders who abused girls had an average of 52 victims each.
  - Only 3% of these crimes had ever been detected.
  - The behavior usually begins in adolescence at the average age of 15.
  - They are the hardest to treat.
  - They are introverted, emotionally immature and fearful of adult heterosexual relationships.
  - They rarely use physical force and are experts at psychological manipulation. Most victims of abuse are "groomed" over a period of weeks, months, or years. Pedophiles are professional con artists and are experts at getting children and families to trust them.
  - They know their victims about 75% of the time and
  - They seek legitimate access to children (families, schools, volunteering, churches, playgrounds, baby-sitting, coaching, hobbies, becoming foster parents, etc.)
  - Pedophiles are notoriously friendly, nice, kind, engaging and likeable.
  - Pedophiles will smile at you, look you right in the eye and make you believe they are trustworthy.

3. Adolescent Offenders[27]
  - 23% of all sexual offenders were under the age of 18.
  - 40% of offenders of victims under age 6 were juveniles
  - 50% of all child sexual abuse is perpetrated by juveniles
  - More often group offenders than adults
  - Often under socialized or pseudo-socialized
  - More sexually aggressive than adults

- Most often molest girls
- 90% are males

When children molest other children, there is a strong correlation that they are victims themselves. Gender is not a distinguishing feature of child to child sexual abuse. Intimidation and force are used. If the child is told the behavior is inappropriate, they will usually continue, but in secret.[28]

Minister's Confession

The following is a letter[29] written by a minister who as part of making restitution wanted to warn parents about the safety of their children. This is for adults and difficult to read. Proceed with caution.

I am a child molester. I have molested more than 80 little girls, ages 4 to 10. For the first time in my life I accept responsibility for my deviancy and criminal activity.

My reason for writing this article is to acquaint you with my tactics, similar to the tactics of other molesters, and to offer suggestions which may assist you in protecting your children from sexual abuse. Angela R. Carl, in Child Abuse, What You Can Do About It, states that a child is molested every two minutes.[30]

For the first time in print, I am exposing my own methods of operation in setting up my victims and how I manipulated the parents, as well as the victims, in order to sexually abuse children. I use the feminine gender because all of my sex-abuse victims are girls. However, the same strategy is used by child molesters who molest boys.

I tell the child our relationship is special. "You are my special little girl. I love you differently than any other little girl." The victim understands that if she tells anyone, the relationship will end.

I remind the child that her dad and mom love me, and they are happy and very pleased that she is my "special little girl." The victim will not wish to disappoint her parents.

I express to the child that I will always continue to do special things for her because of our special relationship and her being my special little girl. Implied is the loss of bribes should she tell.

I also express to the victim that I am making her feel good and she is making me feel good. This creates a belief of dual responsibility. The child believes that she is responsible and will not tell.

I tell the child that we both know that what we are doing is very wrong and ugly, and that no one should ever know. This creates a mutual responsibility so that the victim will not tell.

I cultivate and manipulate the parents and my victim into the relationship. I emphasize to the child, in the presence of her parents, how much I enjoy being able to share a special relationship. Then, vice versa, I tell the parents, in the child's presence, how much I appreciate the child's response to me and the social and spiritual progress I observe in the child. My victim then believes the parents approve of the relationship.

I express to the child how disappointed her parents will be if they know we are doing these "ugly things' together, and I know "we will never tell anyone." Again, the child chooses not to disappoint her family or have them disappointed in her.

I emphasize often to the victim, "You should not let me do this. I love you and I do not want to hurt you, so do not let me do it," knowing that she has no choice. I put the responsibility on the victim, making her think it is her fault, therefore she will not tell.

I say to her, "Just this once, and no more." The child believes it will be the last time. She agrees to experience the uncomfortableness of the situation and will not tell, in order to have the special attention and special favors.

I tell some of my victims that if anyone finds out, I will probably get into trouble, may have to leave and go somewhere else, and may never see her again. I emphasize she may get into trouble also. I continue by saying, "I will miss you and will not be able to do these special things for you." Then I remind her of all the special things I do for her.

It is important to establish an atmosphere of trust at home, so children can and will share experiences in which they are frightened or feel uncomfortable. Once a child has been assaulted, the offender is apt to repeat the offense as often as he can manipulate the situation. I sexually assaulted some victims as much as four dozen times.

Listen to your child. Open communication is the best strategy to protect your child from sexual abuse. A child who has no one to listen to her, or who does not experience love and care, is most vulnerable for sexual exploitation.

I never molested a child who considered me a stranger. I carefully manipulated a trusting relationship, usually with the parents as well as the child. One interaction with a child changes the status of a stranger into a friend. Rather than warn a child about strangers, it would be better to teach her to be aware of actions and behaviors of adults toward her, or situations created by someone showing interest in her.

Become suspicious when someone manipulates trust and begins to shower excessive attention on your child. Confront the adult and inquire as to the motive.

Never force a child to kiss or hug an adult. Respect the child's feelings and allow her to create the boundaries of her relationships with adults. Never force a child to go some place with an adult. If the child is reserved or resistant, she may have good reasons to be.

Always believe your child. If you show the child that you care and are willing to listen, she will usually tell you the truth. Be careful not to overreact, as you may inhibit the child from telling the whole story. If you suspect the child to be lying, allow her to talk. She will contradict herself if she is being dishonest or making up a story. If the child has been sexually abused, do assure her that it is not her fault.

As a child molester, I am most sensitive to a child's vulnerability. I observe children that are emotionally deprived and denied the sense of belonging or being loved. Generally such children will allow me to spend time with them. They will become my special friend and choose to be with me – enduring the bad moments for all the good times we share, to have that sense of being loved and cared for and not alone.

I create an attachment by buying things for a child that she may be deprived of. This establishes an immediate bond and often trust. The child is willing to experience a moment of uncomfortable touching in order to get tangible rewards. A child tends to become attached to anyone who will spend time with her and enjoys the things she enjoys.

Observe your child's behavior and be sensitive to change. A sudden change of behavior such as withdrawal, rebellion, aggression, nightmares, fear of being alone, bedwetting, stomachaches, headaches, genital discomforts, fear of being hugged, sudden drop in grades and/or interest in school, use of sexual talk beyond her maturity level or a desire to run away from home are all possible clues to sexual abuse. A talk with your child may reveal a situation that needs to be addressed and could prevent sexual abuse.

I hope that something I have shared will assist in the prevention of child sexual abuse. I was abused as a child for a period of six years. I trusted no one and was afraid to share with anyone, continuing to endure the abuse.

Take time with your child. It is one of the best investments you can make. Observe your child; it is the best prevention of sexual abuse. BE YOUR CHILD'S BEST FRIEND

Appendix III

Listening Skills

*T*here are two kinds of listening. The first is passive listening which is listening without reacting; allowing someone to speak without interrupting and not doing anything else at the same time. Second, active listening, includes more than passive listening; there is interaction between the speaker and the listener with an acknowledgement that you "hear" them. Becoming an active listener includes three essential components:

1. Pay Attention – look at the speaker, hear their words and focus on their body language. Sitting at eye level with them helps. Listen with your heart, not just your mind. Eye contact is very important. Don't think of what you're going to say next. Remember what they're saying. Make a conscious effort to hear not only the words that another person is saying but, more importantly, try to understand the complete message being sent.
2. Show That You're Listening – nod, smile, use other facial expressions, make sure your posture is open (rather than having your arms crossed), make small comments like "I see" or "yes" or "uh huh."
3. Provide Feedback - Reflect what has been said by paraphrasing. "What I'm hearing is" and "Sounds like you are saying" are great ways to reflect back. Ask questions to clarify certain points. "What do you mean when you say?" "Is this what you mean?" Summarize the speaker's comments periodically. Especially if the speaker is showing emotions either verbally or nonverbally, the active listener can describe the emotion like "You seem sad about that" or "I hear your frustration."

"Active listening gives the speaker the feeling of being understood. This is one of the best feelings in the world - like a breath of fresh air, or a sigh of relief."[31]

Here are some things that active listening is not:

Asking leading questions	Giving advice
Disagreeing	Explaining
Discounting	Changing the subject
Denying the other's feelings	Getting angry
Judging	Lecturing
Analyzing	Problem-solving
Being distracted or bored	Condescending
Placating	Adding your interpretation
Making helpful suggestions	Joking
Comparing	Interrogating
Telling someone how they feel	
Showing the error in their thinking	

To further develop your active listening skills, practice with your spouse, sibling or friend to better prepare yourself for ministering to survivors. Agree with your partner that you will listen for five minutes as they describe some experience they had (even better if it was somewhat emotionally charged). Then ask them to listen to you for five minutes. After you've both shared, talk about the process both as the speaker and the listener. How did it feel to be listened to? What could you do to improve your listening skills?

Appendix IV

PTSD and Flashbacks

*P*osttraumatic stress disorder, or PTSD, can occur after someone goes through, sees, or learns about a traumatic incident. Child sexual or physical abuse and sexual/physical assault are traumatic events.

PTSD has four major symptoms:[32]

1. Reliving the event - Memories of the trauma can come back at any time. You may feel the same fear and horror you did when the event took place. You may have nightmares or feel like you're going through it again. This is called a flashback. Sometimes there is a trigger—a sound or sight that causes you to relive the event.
2. Avoiding situations that remind you of the event - You may try to avoid situations or people that trigger memories of the traumatic event. You may even avoid talking or thinking about the event.
3. Feeling numb - You may find it hard to express your feelings. This is another way to avoid memories. It may also be hard to remember or talk about parts of the trauma. You may find it difficult to experience your emotions. You may not have positive or loving feelings toward other people and may stay away from relationships.
4. Feeling keyed up (also called hyper-arousal) - You may be jittery, or always on the alert and on the lookout for danger. You might suddenly become angry or irritable. This is known as hyper-arousal. You may want to have your back to a wall in a restaurant or waiting room. A loud noise can startle you easily. If someone bumps into you, you might fly into a rage.

Preventing a flashback, if possible, is the best way to handle it. It is often triggered by some kind of reminder of a traumatic event. If you can identify your triggers, then you can avoid them or create a plan to deal with them. It may feel that flashbacks come without warning, but there usually are early warning signs and learning what these are for you is important. Sometimes people get a "fuzzy" feeling or feel like they're withdrawing from people. The more you can detect what your early signs are, the more you can take steps to deal with them.

The goal for handling flashbacks is to get grounded in the present. Here are some things you can do:

- Open your eyes.
- Take slow deep breaths.
- Change your position.
- Look around the room and name objects you see. If possible, say them out loud. Move to a different room or location.
- If possible, be with someone you trust who knows how to help. Go to a safe place.
- Talk about it if you can.
- Let out sound - cry, scream, etc.
- Remind yourself you are experiencing a memory. The event happened in the past. It is not happening now.
- When you are able, journal what you learned from the flashback about yourself, your history, and your present behavior patterns.
- Do not drive or operate machinery until you are fully present.

Appendix V

Self-care for Survivors

1. Talk about it. It's OK to tell.
2. Let go of the guilt. It's not your fault. You could not have stopped it. You did nothing wrong.
3. Express feelings constructively.
   - Talk about what you are feeling
   - Journal
   - Write letters
   - Do something physical: exercise, wring or bite a towel, pound on pillows, scream, kick something soft

4. Confront your abuser by:
   - writing a letter (read to your friend, therapist or group)
   - talking to an empty chair
   - talking at the person's grave
   - Confront directly only if you have no expectation that the person will change or admit abusing you and only when you are clear as to what boundaries you will set with him/her. It is not necessary to directly confront your abuser to heal although if you want to have a relationship with them, it is important.

5. Develop an emergency kit.
   - List of people who care
   - List of phone numbers of support people
   - List of things that have helped in the past
   - Bible verses, poems, and articles that are meaningful to you

- Pets and/or stuffed animals
- Pictures
- Mementoes that lift you up
- List of positives about yourself
- CDs, DVDs, etc. that help you

6. Set boundaries
   - With self, take care of yourself by
     - Taking time for pampering yourself
     - Relax perfectionistic demands on yourself
   - With others, take care of yourself by
     - Saying NO when needed in your caretaker role
     - Saying NO to requests and demands of others
     - Saying NO to being responsible for other's feelings
     - Saying NO to the job of keeping family and friends happy and keeping the "ship afloat."
     - Saying NO to touch you do not want. You have a right to be touched only when you want to be, how you want to be, and only people of your choosing.

7. Learn to enjoy life.
   - Spend time with children and notice how small and vulnerable they are, let your "inner child" play with them
   - Smile at people and compliment someone
   - Get to know other survivors
   - Treat yourself to individual and group therapy
   - Realize you are no longer a victim, you are a survivor on the way to thriving
   - Develop your interests (sewing, quilting, Sudoku, writing, making cards, etc.)
   - Create personal and professional goals
   - Learn to take yourself and life less seriously
   - Learn to do something new
   - Read a book, stories, poems
   - Window shop

8. Physical Self-Care
   - Maintain adequate nutrition
   - Sleep six to eight hours each night
   - Exercise fifteen to twenty minutes a day, three to five times a week – find a kind of exercise you love

- Follow a daily personal care routine
- Avoid junk foods and harmful substances
- Receive weekly therapeutic massages
- Maintain regular physical and dental checkups
- Breathe clean air

9. Spiritual Self-Care
   - Express gratitude for life's gifts
   - Pray, meditate, read inspirational material, etc.
   - Practice compassion and forgiveness for yourself and others
   - Acknowledge humility in not having the "right" answers
   - Spend time in nature, sit in the sun, watch birds and animals, collect stones, watch the stars
   - Express joy
   - Enjoy art - a book, a museum, a gallery, an exhibit
   - Sing, play a musical instrument, listen to music
   - Transform loneliness into quiet and peaceful solitude
   - Experience intimacy and tenderness in relationships with other people
   - Worship God with other believers in a safe space

Appendix VI

Biblical Names/Descriptions for God

- Alpha, Almighty, Awesome, Adored, Advocate, Ancient of Days, Author, Anchor, Amen, Adonai, Abba, Anointed One
- Beginning, Bread of Life, Breath, Bridegroom, Blessed, Beloved, Burden-Bearer, Barrier-Breaker, Boundless, Bountiful, Branch, Bruised, Beautiful, Beloved
- Christ, Creator, Counselor, Carpenter, Captain, Conqueror, Crowned, Companion, Center, Cornerstone, Compassionate, Comforter, Crucified, Chosen One, Consuming Fire,
- Dwelling, Deliverer, Defender, Delight, Desire of All Nations, Door, Day-Spring, Divine
- Emmanuel, El Shaddai, Everlasting Father, Eternal, Encourager, Example, Exalted, Elohim, Enduring, End, Enthroned, Exalted,
- Father, Friend, Fellow, Fountain, Fire, Forgiving, Faithful and True, Fairest, Finisher, Fullness, Foundation
- Guide, Guardian, Good, Great, Gatherer, Glorious, Gracious, Gift, Giver, Gardener, Goal, Gate, God Who Sees Me
- Holy One, Highest, Hallowed, Hiding Place, Heart-Broken, Husband, Hope, Healer, Helper, Hand, Home, Holy Spirit, High Priest, Heir of All Things, Horn of Salvation
- I AM, Incarnate Word, Instructor, Immortal, Incomprehensible, Incomparable, Infinite, Invisible, Infallible, Invincible, Ineffable, Indwelling, Intercessor, Inspirer
- Jehovah, Judge, Just, Justifier, Jealous, Joy, Jesus
- King, Kinsman, Keeper, Kind, Key

- Lamb of God, Lord, Light of the World, Life, Love, Leader, Long-Suffering, Lowly, Listener, Lawgiver, Like an Eagle, Lily of the Valleys, Living Stone, Living Water, Lord of Glory, Lord of Hosts
- Messiah, Maker, Most High, Master, Mighty, Meek, Mediator, Merciful, Measureless, Majesty, Mindful, Manna, Mysterious, Morning Star, Man of Sorrows
- Needed, Nearest, Nourisher, Nurturer
- Omniscient, Omnipresent, Omnipotent, Only-Begotten, Owner, Overcomer, Omega
- Prophet, Priest, Prince of Peace, Physician, Patient, Peace, Purest Pleasure, Protector, Provider, Preserver, Possessor, Precious, Pastor, Perfect, Priceless, Prince of Peace, Praiseworthy, Pioneer, Prize, Pardoning, Persistent, Pearl, Pure, Purifier, Prayer-Hearer, Potter
- Quickener, Queller-of-Storms, Quietness
- Redeemer, Resurrection, Refiner, Refuge, Righteous, Righteousness, Rule, Radiant, Reprover, Reformer, Renewer, Ransom, Refresher, Rescuer, Receiver, Road, Rewarder, Ruler, Restorer, Rock, Rest, Rod, Rich, Rabboni (Teacher), Refiner's Fire, Rose of Sharon
- Son, Son of Man, Servant, Savior, Shepherd, Sacrifice, Salvation, Splendor, Spirit, Satisfaction, Satisfier, Source, Spring, Sanctification, Sanctifier, Stronghold, Strength, Strengthener, Sun, Shield, Steadfast, Sufficient, Skillful, Strong, Supreme, Shade, Silent, Star, Song Seeker, Sovereign, Slow-to-Anger, Sanctuary, Sower, Seed of the Woman
- Triumphant, Transcendent, Transformer, Teacher, Treasure, Treasury, Truth, True, Tender, Tower, Trustworthy, Truth, Trinity, Three in One
- Uncreated Light, Unchangeable, Understanding, Undefeated, Unhurried, Unfailing, Unhindered, Unwearied, Unlimited, Uplifter, Upholder
- Vine, Vindicator, Vision, Visible, Veil, Vanquisher, Verity, Victory, Voice
- Way, Water of Life, Word, Wine, Wisdom, Wonderful, Well-Spring, Worthy, Wise, Watcher, Wounded
- Yahweh, Yours, Yearning, Yearned-for, Yokefellow

Appendix VII

Domestic Violence Information

*O*ne in four women in the Christian community is being abused by a partner or has experienced abuse at some time in the past. How many does that make in your congregation? Don't be fooled by everything looking good. It is happening more often than we know. Approximately 1,500 women are killed each year by husbands or boyfriends. About 2 million men per year beat their partners. This is a very serious situation and the more we know, the more able we are to bring hope and healing to the women and men caught up in this tragedy. Although not all domestic violence victims are women in marriage relationships, about 90% are. In this information section, I will refer to the victim as a woman and the abuser as a man.

What are the warning signs?[33]

There are some telltale signs and symptoms of emotional abuse and domestic violence. If you witness any of these warning signs of abuse, take them very seriously.

Women who are being abused may:

- Seem afraid or overly anxious to please him.
- Go along with everything he says and does.
- Check in often with him to report where they are and what they're doing.
- Receive frequent, harassing phone calls from him.
- Talk about his temper, jealousy, or possessiveness.
- Have frequent injuries, with the excuse of "accidents."

- Dress in clothing designed to hide bruises or scars (e.g. wearing long sleeves in the summer or sunglasses indoors).
- Have very low self-esteem, even if they used to be confident.
- Show major personality changes (e.g. an outgoing person becomes withdrawn).
- Be depressed, anxious, or suicidal.

People who are being isolated by their abuser may:

- Be restricted from seeing family and friends.
- Rarely go out in public without their partner.
- Have limited access to money, credit cards, or the car.

Who are the abusers?

Domestic violence crosses all social, economic and religious boundaries. There is no "typical" abuser. In public, they may appear friendly and loving to their partner and family. They often only abuse behind closed doors. They also try to hide the abuse by causing injuries that can be hidden and do not need a doctor.

Many people think of domestic violence abusers as being out of control, crazy, and unpredictable, the contrary is often true. The violence used by abusers is controlled and manipulative. They believe they have a right to control their wives. Their need to control is far greater than their capacity for love of their spouse or the children. They minimize the impact and effect of their abuse. This minimization of the abuse makes their partners feel they are over-reacting. They blame their partner for the abuse and may blame alcohol, drugs, their parents, their job, their church, or anything to justify their behavior.

Subtle red flags that characterize many abusers include:[34]

- They insist on moving too quickly into a relationship.
- They can be very charming and may seem too good to be true.
- They insist their partner stop participating in leisure activities or spending time with family and friends.
- They are extremely jealous or controlling.
- They do not take responsibility for their actions and blame others for everything that goes wrong.
- They criticize their partner's appearance and make frequent put-downs.
- Their words and actions don't match.

Common Beliefs of Abusers include:

- Anger causes violence
- Women are manipulative
- If I don't control her, she'll control me
- Smashing things isn't abusive, it's venting
- Sometimes there's no alternative to violence
- Women are just as abusive as men
- Women want to be dominated by men
- Somebody has to be in charge
- Jealousy is natural to men
- Violence is a breakdown in communications
- Men can't change if women won't
- In Christian circles, we can add:
  - o Women are supposed to be submissive.
  - o She must obey me; I'm the head of the house.
  - o I'm just following Ephesians 5:22.

What is the Cycle of Abuse?

Lenore Walker, a psychologist, found that many violent relationships follow a common pattern or cycle.[35] The entire cycle may happen in one day or it may take weeks or months. Although it is a common pattern, not all couples follow it exactly.

This cycle has three parts:

- Tension building phase—Tension builds expressed by poor communication, passive aggression, rising interpersonal tension, and fear of causing outbursts in one's partner. During this stage she may attempt to modify her behavior to avoid triggering his outburst. None of these will stop the violence. Eventually, the tension reaches a boiling point and physical abuse begins.
- Acute battering episode—when the tension peaks, the physical violence begins. It is usually triggered by the presence of an external event or by his emotional state—but not by her behavior. This means the start of the battering episode is unpredictable and beyond her control.
- The honeymoon phase—first, the abuser is ashamed of his behavior. He expresses remorse, tries to minimize the abuse and might even blame it on himself. He may then exhibit loving, kind behavior followed by apologies, generosity and helpfulness. He will genuinely attempt to con-

vince her that the abuse will not happen again. This loving and contrite behavior strengthens the bond between the partners and will probably convince her, once again, that leaving the relationship is not necessary.

This cycle continues over and over, and may help explain why she stays in the abusive relationship. The abuse may be terrible, but the promises and generosity of the honeymoon phase give her the false belief that everything will be all right. In later stages of abuse, however, the honeymoon phase is often absent.

Why does the abused partner stay?

While most battered women eventually leave their abusers, a quarter to a third, remain in their abusive relationships. There are a variety of reasons. Here are a few of them:

- *Love* – she loves him. After all, he is not always violent. He tells her that he'll change and she wants to believe him. She wants the violence to stop, not for the relationship to end.
- *Fear* - She fears him, believing him to be almost "godlike." He may threaten over and over that he will hurt her, their children, a pet, a family member, a friend or himself. She may stay in the relationship because she is scared of what he will do if she leaves. Many states have little or no protection for a battered wife. Even states that have protection may not enforce the law consistently especially if he is believable and denies the abuse.
- *Low self-esteem* - When he calls her names, puts her down and plays mind games it can make her feel bad about herself. She may rationalize the abuse, believing that she must have "deserved" it.
- *Financial* - She may not leave because she is scared that she will not have enough money to support herself - a fear that often gets worse if she has children. Abusers set up the finances to keep her from having access to family funds.
- *Believing Abuse is Normal*: She may have lived in a home in which one parent beat the other and/or the children and sees violence as an inevitable part of the way in which couples relate. Or, she may have lived in a home where the wife was submissive to the husband, but there was no abuse. She believes if she was a better wife the abuse wouldn't happen.
- *Religious or Social* – She may be influenced by her church or pastor to stay rather than end the relationship because that is what God wants. He is usually very charming, talented and believable. People have a hard

time believing he would do such a thing. They think she is exaggerating and perhaps needs to pray more, exhibit a more submissive spirit or use Abigail as an example.

Why is domestic violence also spiritually abusive?

Spiritual abuse tactics[36] can inflict considerable harm on victims of domestic violence, making them question their spiritual values and beliefs. Here are some examples of spiritual abuse used by perpetrators:

- Abusers cite scripture to justify abusive, dominating or oppressive behavior.
- Abusers deny their partners the freedom to practice the religion of their choice.
- Abusers force their partners to violate their religious beliefs.
- Abusers shame or belittle their partners for their religious practices.
- Abusers make oppressive demands based on their interpretation of scriptures or other religious teachings (e.g., "the scriptures say that you need to obey me because you are my wife").
- Abusers instill religious guilt in victims for not doing what they want them to do (e.g., "How can you call yourself religious if you don't forgive me?").
- Abusers' sense of marital entitlement causes them to justify their sexual demands, including forced sex (i.e., marital rape).
- Abusers manipulate others in their religious communities to control and ostracize their partners.

Counseling Suggestions:[37]

- Joint counseling is not recommended until the domestic violence is dealt with fully because:
  - Domestic violence is not the same as marriage relationship issues. It is an individual issue for him, first and foremost. Fixing communication patterns, etc. won't work and puts the onus on her to control the violence, something she can't do.
  - Anger management alone does not work; it also puts the burden on her to change her behavior so she doesn't provoke him.
  - It inhibits her freedom to talk honestly.
  - It gives him power over her through silent threats and manipulations.
  - It puts her in danger of retaliation after the counseling session.

- Things to keep in mind if she comes to you for help:
    - o Don't miss the warning signs – She may come to you thinking she is the one who needs help with being more submissive or "obedient." Just because she doesn't see herself as abused doesn't mean she's not. She may be ashamed to tell you about what's happening and may want to protect his reputation. Domestic violence is a big secret. Asking some specific questions helps:[61]
        - Do you ever feel frightened of him?
        - What happens when you express an opinion different from his?
        - Has he ever slapped or pushed you, hit or threatened you?
    - o Believe her– assume she is telling the truth even if he is a church leader or large contributor to the church.
    - o Understand she is minimizing her experience - she is likely only giving you a small glimpse of the real situation to see how you will react.
    - o Assess her safety needs– Take threats seriously and remember that verbal abuse is equally as destructive as physical violence.
    - o Don't place the focus on her behavior – focus instead on her safety and physical, emotional and spiritual health. Name the abuse, call it by its right name; sin against God and her.
    - o Don't hold her responsible for keeping the family together – the breakup is not her fault. She should not be blamed for seeking safety. She should not be advised to stay when safety is at stake.
    - o Don't refuse to believe he could do such a thing – Most abusers present themselves as congenial, spiritual and devoted to their families. But, they are master manipulators who use Scripture to justify their use of power and control to "save the family for God."
    - o Don't contact the abuser to tell him about his wife's visit without her permission or having a safety plan in place – she is put at great physical danger.
    - o Don't confront the abuser alone – Follow Matthew 18 and always have someone with you. Make sure there is a safety plan in place for you, the church and her. Have a plan in place for him to get help.
    - o Don't assume the abuser will change if he repents of his sin – his repentance may be genuine, but there are still consequences to actions and work for him to do. The only way to know if change is genuine is over a period of time.
    - o Don't devalue a structured separation or promote reconciliation too soon – if he has truly changed, he will be willing to wait and do the work necessary. Don't encourage reconciliation too soon. Many treatment programs recommend a minimum of six months of treatment and an additional six months of follow-up. Research indicates that

50% of court-appointed offenders will recidivate within five years. If he has truly changed, he will be willing to wait in order to build trust. He will respect her boundaries in every situation. He will need an accountability structure, probably for the rest of his life.

What are resources available to victims?

Victims have many options, from obtaining a protection order to staying in a shelter, or exploring options through support group or anonymous calls to a local domestic violence shelter or hotline program. There is hope for victims, and they are not alone. There are thousands of local shelters across the United States that provide safety, counseling, legal help, and other resources for victims and their children.[38]

- If you are in danger, call 911, a local hotline or a national hotline.
- www.nnedv.org National Network to End Domestic Violence website has safety tips and resources
- www.ndvh.org National Domestic Violence Hotline
  800-799-SAFE /800-799-7233 and 800-787-3224 (TTY).
  24-hour-a-day hotline, Provides crisis intervention and referrals to local services and shelters for victims of partner or spousal abuse. English and Spanish speaking advocates are available 24 hours a day, seven days a week. It is staffed by trained volunteers who are ready to connect people with emergency help in their own communities, including emergency services and shelters.
- www.loveisrepect.org
  U.S. National Teen Dating Abuse Hotline: Phone: 1-866-331-9474
- www.womenslaw.org
  Women's Law has legal information and resources for victims
- www.clicktoempower.com
  The Allstate Foundation has resources to end financial abuse.
- http://www.focusministries1.org
  FOCUS Ministries is devoted to offering hope, encouragement, education, and assistance to women and families who are struggling in difficult circumstances, especially dysfunctional marriages, spousal abuse (domestic violence), separation, or divorce.

NOTE: Before using online resources, know that your computer or phone may not be safe. Some abusers are misusing technology to stalk and track all of a partner's activities.

Appendix VIII

Sexual Assault Information

*T*he following information on sexual assault is taken from the U. S. Department of Health and Human Services Office on Women's Health.[39]

What is sexual assault?

Sexual assault and abuse is any type of sexual activity that you do not agree to, including:

- Inappropriate touching
- Vaginal, anal, or oral penetration
- Sexual intercourse that you say no to
- Rape
- Attempted rape
- Child molestation

Sexual assault can be verbal, visual, or anything that forces a person to join in unwanted sexual contact or attention. Examples of this are voyeurism (when someone watches private sexual acts), exhibitionism (when someone exposes him/herself in public), incest (sexual contact between family members), and sexual harassment. It can happen in different situations: in the home by someone you know, on a date, or by a stranger in an isolated place.

Rape is a common form of sexual assault. It is committed in many situations — on a date, by a friend or an acquaintance, or when you think you are alone. Educate yourself on "date rape" drugs. They can be slipped into a drink when a victim is not looking. Never leave your drink unattended — no matter where you are. Attackers use date rape drugs to make a person unable to resist assault. These drugs can also cause memory loss so the victim doesn't know what happened. Rape and sexual assault are never the victim's fault — no matter where or how it happens.

What do I do if I've been sexually assaulted?

These are important steps to take right away after an assault:

- Get away from the attacker to a safe place as fast as you can. Then call 911 or the police.
- Call a friend or family member you trust. You also can call a crisis center or a hotline to talk with a counselor. One hotline is the National Sexual Assault Hotline at 800-656-HOPE (4673). Feelings of shame, guilt, fear, and shock are normal. It is important to get counseling from a trusted professional.
- Do not wash, comb, or clean any part of your body. Do not change clothes if possible, so the hospital staff can collect evidence. Do not touch or change anything at the scene of the assault.
- Go to your nearest hospital emergency room as soon as possible. You need to be examined, treated for any injuries, and screened for possible sexually transmitted infections (STIs) or pregnancy. The doctor will collect evidence using a rape kit for fibers, hairs, saliva, semen, or clothing that the attacker may have left behind.
- While at the hospital:
  - o If you decide you want to file a police report, you or the hospital staff can call the police from the emergency room.
  - o Ask the hospital staff to connect you with the local rape crisis center. The center staff can help you make choices about reporting the attack and getting help through counseling and support groups.

How can I lower my risk of sexual assault?

There are things you can do to reduce your chances of being sexually assaulted. Follow these tips from the National Crime Prevention Council.

- Be aware of your surroundings — who's out there and what's going on.
- Walk with confidence. The more confident you look, the stronger you appear.
- Know your limits when it comes to using alcohol.
- Be assertive — don't let anyone violate your space.

- Trust your instincts. If you feel uncomfortable in your surroundings, leave.
- Don't prop open self-locking doors.
- Lock your door and your windows, even if you leave for just a few minutes.
- Watch your keys. Don't lend them. Don't leave them. Don't lose them. And don't put your name and address on the key ring.
- Watch out for unwanted visitors. Know who's on the other side of the door before you open it.
- Be wary of isolated spots, like underground garages, offices after business hours, and apartment laundry rooms.
- Avoid walking or jogging alone, especially at night. Vary your route. Stay in well-traveled, well-lit areas.
- Have your key ready to use before you reach the door — home, car, or work.
- Park in well-lit areas and lock the car, even if you'll only be gone a few minutes.
- Drive on well-traveled streets, with doors and windows locked.
- Never hitchhike or pick up a hitchhiker.
- Keep your car in good shape with plenty of gas in the tank.
- In case of car trouble, call for help on your cellular phone. If you don't have a phone, put the hood up, lock the doors, and put a banner in the rear window that says, "Help. Call police."

How can I help someone who has been sexually assaulted?

You can help someone who has been assaulted by listening and offering comfort. Go with her or him to the police, the hospital, or to counseling. Reinforce the message that she or he is not at fault and that it is natural to feel angry and ashamed.

Where else can I go for help?

If you are sexually assaulted, it is not your fault. Don't be afraid to ask for help or support. Help is available. There are many organizations and hotlines in every state and territory. These crisis centers and agencies work hard to stop assaults and help victims. You also can obtain the numbers of shelters, counseling services, and legal assistance in your phone book or online.

You can call these organizations:

- National Domestic Violence Hotline 800-799-SAFE (7233) or 800-787-3224 (TDD)
- National Sexual Assault Hotline 800-656-HOPE (4673)

For more information about sexual assault, go to womenshealth.gov, call 800-994-9662 (TDD: 888-220-5446) or contact the following organizations:

- Loveisrespect.org –
  Phone: 866-331-9474 (TDD: 866-331-8453)
- National Center for Victims of Crime
  Phone: 800-394-2255 or 202-467-8700 (TDD: 800-211-7996)
- National Crime Prevention Council
  Phone: 202-466-6272
- National Sexual Violence Resource Center (NSVRC)
  Phone: 877-739-3895 or 717-909-0710 (TDD: 717-909-0715)
- Office on Violence Against Women, OJP, DOJ
  Phone: 202-307-6026 (TDD: 202-307-2277)
- Rape, Abuse, and Incest National Network (RAINN)
  Phone: 800-656-4673 or 202-544-1034

Appendix IX

Guidelines for
Finding a Therapist

General Information about Therapists

- There are different kinds of therapist with different degrees, licensures and functions.
- Psychiatrists are medical doctors who diagnose and treat emotional and mental health issues. They are the only practitioners who can prescribe medication.
- Psychologists have a doctorate in psychology. They can diagnose mental and emotional health problems and offer counseling services but cannot prescribe medications.
- Psychiatric Nurses are certified nurses who have received additional training in the treatment and diagnosis of emotional and mental health problems.
- Clinical Social Workers have earned a masters degree and have been trained in making mental health diagnoses and offering counseling services. They must have state licensure.
- Licensed Professional Counselor (or Mental Health Counselor) have a masters degree in counseling or in a related field and can provide counseling services. They must have state licensure.
- Drug and Alcohol (Addictions) counselors have a university degree and have received additional specialized training in addiction counseling. Addictions counselors can diagnose addiction problems and can offer individual and group therapy. They should have a state license to practice.

- Marriage or Family Therapists have a masters degree or higher in counseling or a related field and have received specialized training in marriage and family counseling.
- Art Therapists have a masters degree in art therapy or a related field and will use creative pursuits like painting or sculpture to help express deep seated emotions. (Music Therapists are similar, but use music as the creative way to deal with emotions.)
- Religious or Pastoral Counselors are members of the clergy who have received some training in counseling.

General Information about Types of Therapy

*T*herapy can be delivered in different ways like individual, family, marriage or group therapy. There are dozens of types of therapy. Many therapists are eclectic and use a variety of methods. Christian therapists may also use a variety of methods in the context of a biblically-based Christ centered therapy. Here are a few of the major modalities that are helpful to abuse survivors.

- Addiction Recovery Therapy - addresses the symptoms of addictions and related areas of impaired functioning and the content and structure of the client's ongoing recovery program. This model is a time-limited approach that focuses on behavioral change, usually includes 12-step focus, tools for recovery and self-help participation. Can be given in individual or group therapy.
- Anger Management - a process of learning to recognize signs that you're becoming angry and taking action to calm down and deal with the situation in a positive way. Can be given in the context of a class, group or individual therapy.
- Body Therapies – involves working with the human body to connect body and mind. It is helpful because memories are stored in the body and can often be resolved through bodywork. A type of body therapy, bioenergetics, is a form of psychodynamic psychotherapy that combines work with the body and mind to help people resolve their emotional problems and realize more of their potential for joy in living. Deep tissue massage and biofeedback are also part of body therapies.
- Cognitive Behavioral Therapy (CBT) - a type of psychotherapeutic treatment that helps patients understand the thoughts and feelings that influence behaviors. CBT is commonly used to treat a wide range of disorders, including phobias, addiction, depression and anxiety. It is generally short-term and focused on helping clients deal with a very specific problem. It's very helpful with changing false beliefs.

- Eye Movement Desensitization and Reprocessing (EMDR) – is a therapy where a patient brings to mind emotionally unpleasant images and beliefs about themselves related to their traumatic event. With these thoughts and images in mind, patients are asked to also pay attention to an outside stimulus, such as eye movements or finger tapping guided by the therapist. The goal is to reprocess trauma/abuse and connect right and left brain; front and back brain which is dissociated during the trauma. This therapy is listed in the new Department of Veterans Affairs & Department of Defense Practice Guidelines as "highly recommended" for the treatment of trauma (PTSD).
- Expressive Therapies – includes art, music, sand tray, drama, movement, journaling, etc. Encourages expression in a safe therapeutic environment. Can be given in individual or group sessions.
- Grief Therapy - refers to a specific form of therapy, or a focus in general counseling with the goal of helping the individual grieve and address personal loss in a healthy manner. Grief counseling is offered individually or in groups by counselors or clergy, as well as informal support groups offered by churches, community groups, or organizations devoted to helping individuals grieve specific losses.

How Do I Choose a Therapist?

1. Pray about it. The Holy Spirit knows what kind of therapy you need and just the person you need to work with. Ask for wisdom from above in making your decision.
2. Know your specific needs and seek out a therapist with specific experience with your issue. What do you need to work on? Is it relationship issues? Do you need to address the false beliefs you have. Do you feel numb and want to be more alive in your body? Do you want to deal directly with the trauma of the abuse? Brainstorm in your journal about what you need; then explore the section on General Information about Therapists.
3. If you don't find out before, ask questions at your first session. You're interviewing the therapist as much as they are interviewing you. Ask them if they have seen a lot of clients with your same concerns. Ask them when was the last time they treated someone with a problem like yours. A good therapist will welcome those questions.
4. Choose someone with experience. Research doesn't show much difference between the quality of therapy outcomes based upon a clinician's degree or training, but it does show that the longer a clinician has been practicing, the better client outcomes will be.

5. Get referrals from satisfied customers. Ask fellow survivors about their recommendations. Ask other safe people for their experiences.

6. Ask the Question: "Have you done your own work?" A therapist who has done their work will welcome this question. You want someone who has dealt with their own psychological issues and knows what it's like to do tough emotional work. The therapist doesn't need to share what that work is, but they should be able to reassure you that they know what that means.

7. Inquire whether the therapist is involved with ongoing education and/or supervision. If the therapist is licensed (and they should be), they will be involved in continuing education (CEUs). Supervision means the therapist has another professional that they talk to about their client work so they keep their own issues from interfering with the therapy.

8. Seek someone who doesn't ask a lot of leading questions. Most of the time you don't want someone that dictates what happens in your therapy space. You need this space to work on your agenda, not a dictated one. There are some therapies, however, that by their very nature are very structured like CBT and EMDR and they have their place.

9. Seek someone who helps you find the answers to your questions. Advice giving is not a good therapeutic technique. Most of the time you need the space to search and find your own answers and God's answers for you. Having someone tell you how you should or should not feel and/or what the answers are is not very helpful and stunts your emotional growth.

10. You owe it to yourself to feel comfortable and safe with your therapist. Therapy is not an easy process and while your therapist is not there to be your friend, you can certainly choose a therapist whom you feel respects your individuality, opinions, and self. You must be able to trust your therapist and if you cannot and feel like you have to lie to your therapist or withhold important information, you are not going to get any real help.

11. Choose someone you can afford. Check to see if they are on your insurance. If you don't have insurance, there are several places you can find a good therapist. Check with churches who offer counseling. Just make sure the person is qualified with the proper preparation to do counseling. Check with the county mental health department, they often have some very good counselors. Check with other non-profit therapy agencies in your area who may work on a sliding fee scale.

Appendix X

Suicide Prevention Guidelines

S uicide is a serious problem. It is the tenth leading cause of death. Every 13.7 minutes someone in the United States dies from suicide. Nearly 1,000,000 people have attempted suicide in the last year. The suicide rate is the highest it's been in the last fifteen years. Men are nearly four times more likely to die from suicide than women because they choose more lethal methods. Women are three times more likely to attempt suicide.

When someone says he or she is thinking about suicide, or says things that sounds as if the person is considering suicide, here's what to do:

1. Tell the person you are concerned and give him/her examples.
2. Ask questions. Be sensitive but be direct. Asking about suicidal thoughts and feelings won't push someone into doing something harmful. Instead, offering someone an opportunity to speak about their thoughts and feelings may decrease the risk of acting on the suicidal thoughts and feelings. Here are some questions to ask.
   a. How are you coping?
   b. Do you ever feel like giving up?
   c. Are you thinking about hurting yourself?
   d. Are you thinking about dying?
   e. Are you thinking about suicide?
   f. Have you thought about how you would do it?
   g. Do you know when you would do it?
   h. Do you have the means to do it?

3. Be willing to listen.
   a. Do not attempt to argue someone out of suicide. Rather, let the person know you care, that he/she is not alone, that suicidal feelings are temporary and that depression can be treated. Don't try to talk the person out of his or her feelings or express shock. Avoid the temptation to say, "You have so much to live for," or "Your suicide will hurt your family."
   b. Encourage the person to communicate with you. Someone who's suicidal may be tempted to bottle up feelings because he or she feels ashamed, guilty or embarrassed. Be supportive and understanding, and express your opinions without placing blame. Listen attentively and avoid interrupting.

4. Seek professional help.
   a. Be actively involved in encouraging the person to see a physician or mental health professional immediately. Someone who is suicidal or has severe depression may not have the energy or motivation to find help.
   b. Never promise to keep someone's suicidal feelings a secret. Be understanding, but explain that you may not be able to keep such a promise if you think the person's life is in danger. At that point, you have to get help.
   c. Individuals contemplating suicide often don't believe they can be helped, so you may have to do more.
   d. Help the person find a knowledgeable mental health professional or a reputable treatment facility, and take them to the treatment.

5. Know the risk factors.
   a. Ninety percent of people who kill themselves have a diagnosable and treatable mental illness – major depression, PTSD, anxiety disorder, bulimia, anorexia, alcohol or drug abuse, etc.
   b. Previous attempts
   c. Having a plan
   d. Genetic predisposition
   e. Neurotransmitters – there is a clear relationship between low concentrations of serotonin and attempted and/or completed suicides
   f. Major loss or other precipitating event
   g. Hopelessness

6. Look for warning signs. You can't always tell when someone is considering suicide, but here are some common signs:
   a. Talking about it. "I wish I were dead." "I wish I hadn't been born." "I'm going to kill myself." "My family would be better off without me."
   b. Signs of depression like: anxiety, pain, social withdrawal, sleep or eating changes, pessimism, hopelessness, desperation, mood swings (being emotionally high one day and deeply depressed the next), being preoccupied with death, dying or violence
   c. Increasing the use of alcohol and/or drugs
   d. Making a plan:
      • Giving away belongings and getting affairs in order without a logical explanation as to why they are doing so
      • Saying goodbye to people as if they'll never see them again
      • Sudden or impulsive purchase of a firearm
      • Obtaining other means of killing oneself such as poisons or medications
   e. Unexpected rage or anger

7. Get emergency help. If you believe someone is in danger of committing suicide or has made a suicide attempt:
   a. Don't leave them alone.
   b. Remove from the vicinity any firearms, drugs or sharp objects that could be used for suicide.
   c. Take the person to an emergency room or walk-in clinic at a psychiatric hospital.
   d. If a psychiatric facility is unavailable, go to your nearest hospital or clinic.
   e. If the above options are unavailable, call 911 or the National Suicide Prevention Lifeline at 1-800-273-TALK (8255).

8. You're not responsible for preventing someone from taking his or her own life — but your intervention may help the person see that other options are available to stay safe and get treatment.

Appendix XI

Resources

Abuse Recovery - Christian

www.hopeforhurtinghearts.com
Resources for healing from abuse of all types

www.spiritualabuse.com
Resources for those who have experienced spiritual abuse

www.thehopeofsurvivors.com
Support, hope and healing for victims of pastoral sexual abuse

www.recoveryfromabuse.com
A practical introduction for pastors and other religious professionals

www.christiansurvivors.com
An active community of survivors of all types of abuse – a safe oasis to provide friendship, understanding, and support to survivors of all forms of abuse

www.christianrecovery.com
Helping the Christian community become a safe place for people recovering
from addiction, abuse, or trauma

Abuse Recovery

www.soul-expressions-abuse-recovery.com
Resources for psychotherapists and others who have survived child abuse and other trauma, includes a variety of useful links for both survivors and counselors

www.overcomingsexualabuse.com
Overcoming Sexual Abuse inspires, empowers, educates & supports male and female survivors of sexual abuse

Addiction Recovery – Christian

www.overcomersoutreach.org
A Christ-centered 12-Step recovery program that addresses addictions & compulsions - bridges the gap between traditional 12-Step support groups and hurting people in churches of all denominations

www.confidentkids.com
A special program with groups designed to help children from addicted and dysfunctional families

www.prodigalsinternational.org
Christ-centered 12-Step sexual addiction recovery support groups for men. Partners in Process is the Prodigals program for the spouses of sex addicts

www.celebraterecovery.com
Celebrate Recovery is a program designed to help those struggling with hurts, hang-ups, and habits by showing them the loving power of Jesus Christ through the recovery process

www.christianrecoveryonline.net
Christian Recovery Online is a place for Christians in recovery and all Christians to meet online and socialize with other Christians. Based on Celebrate Recovery

www.christiancodependence.com
Information and resources on codependence for Christians

www.christians-in-recovery.org
Information, tools, and resources for those seeking recovery from life's trials, problems, addictions and dysfunctions

www.nacr.org
National Association for Christian Recovery has a passion to cultivate and grow recovery communities within or in partnership with Christian churches - for people in recovery, their family, pastor, recovery ministry leader or mental health professional

www.clergyrecovery.com
The Clergy Recovery Network exists to support, encourage and provide resources to religious professionals in recovery – for pastors, missionaries, religious professionals or spouses

Addiction Recovery

www.adultchildren.org
Adult Children of Alcoholics is an anonymous Twelve Step program of women and men who grew up in an alcoholic or otherwise dysfunctional home

www.coda.org
Co-Dependents Anonymous, a fellowship of men and women whose common purpose is to develop healthy relationships

www.al-anon.org
Official web site, has a comprehensive listing of meeting information in the U.S. and Canada

www.alladdictsanonymous.org
A program of recovery for all addicts and all addictions

www.soberrecovery.com
Thousands of recovery links for when you need help, for alcoholism or addiction, dual diagnosis, treatment, sober living, sex addiction and recovery, gambling, overeating, mental illness - for anything life throws at you

Abuse Hotlines

www.allaboutcounseling.com/crisis_hotlines.htm
Many helplines listed along with descriptions of the services they provide

www.avhotline.org/abuse/hotlines/index.html
Abuse Victim Hotline - abuse hotline listed for each state and many links for all kinds of abuse help, a place to click for confidential IM service, and a place to connect to free legal counsel and advice

www.rainn.org
Rape, Abuse & Incest National Network (RAINN) - The nation's largest anti-sexual violence organization – information, help, statistics and prevention
National Sexual Assault Hotline 1-800-656-HOPE

www.childhelp.org
Child Abuse Hotline – anonymous and confidential 24/7 professional crisis counselors, assistance in 170 languages; offers crisis intervention, information, literature, and referrals to thousands of emergency, social service, and support resources
US or Canada: 1-800-4-A-CHILD (1-800-422-4453)

www.stopitnow.org
Stop It Now – focused on preventing the sexual abuse of children by mobilizing adults, families and communities to take actions that protect children before they are harmed
Helpline for questions and concerns - 1-888-PREVENT (1-888-773-8368)

www.ChiWorld.org
List of international child helplines

http://www.nccafv.org/state_elder_abuse_hotlines.htm
Elder Abuse Hotline - National Council on Child Abuse and Family Violence (NCCAFV) – if you suspect elder abuse, call your state's elder abuse hotline (listen on the website) or 1-800-677-1116, available from Monday through Friday 9 AM-8 PM (except U.S. federal holidays)

www.suicidehotlines.com
National Suicide Hotlines – List of suicide hotlines for all the states and national numbers - Toll-Free 24/7
1-800-SUICIDE (1-800-784-2433)
1-800-273-TALK (1-800-273-8255)
1-800-799-4TTY (4889) – for the deaf

Boys Town Suicide and Crisis Line: 800-448-3000 or 800-448-1833 (TDD) 24/7 short-term crisis intervention and counseling and referrals to local community resources; counseling on parent-child conflicts, marital and family issues, suicide, pregnancy, runaway youth, physical and sexual abuse, and other issues

Books

Abuse

1. Ewert, Heyward Bruce III and Lawrence Stevenson. *AM I BAD? Recovering From Abuse*. Ann Arbor, MI: Loving Healing Press, 2007

   If you were abused or neglected as a child, chances are that you have been your whole life, whether you are a man, a woman, or a teen. Child abuse so mangles the personality that the victim unconsciously attracts abusers throughout the life cycle.

2. Gil, Eliana. *Outgrowing the Pain: A Book for and About Adults Abused As Children*. New York: Dell Publishing, 1988.

   This much-needed book pinpoints the typical problems abused children experience when they become adults. The information is presented in a friendly and thorough manner for victims and professionals. (Also Outgrowing the Pain Together)

3. Tracy, Steven. *Mending the Soul: Understanding and Healing Abuse*. Grand Rapids, MI: Zondervan, 2008.

   This book provides a well-researched biblical and scientific overview of abuse. A broad overview, it deals with the various types of abuse, the various effects of abuse, and the means of healing.

Emotional Abuse

1. Jantz, Gregory and Ann McMurray. *Healing the Scars of Emotional Abuse*. Grand Rapids, MI: Revell Publishing, 2009

   In spite of their physical invisibility, emotional wounds are a very damaging form of abuse. Whether caused by words, actions, or even indifference, emotional abuse is common—yet often overlooked. In this helpful guide, Dr. Gregory L. Jantz through scriptural and biblically oriented guidance reveals how those who have been abused by a spouse, parent, employer, or minister can overcome the past and rebuild their self-image.

2. Paul, Christi. *Love Isn't Supposed to Hurt*. Carol Stream, IL Tyndale House Books, 2012.

   Written with great candor and poignancy, Love Isn't Supposed to Hurt chronicles Christi's personal experience of dealing with emotional abuse and shows how—with God's help, some unconventional therapy, and the support of family and friends—she was able to break the cycle of abuse, regain her sense of self-worth, and discover what true love is really all about.

Sexual Abuse

1. Allender, Dan. *The Wounded Heart: Hope for Adult Victims of Childhood Sexual Abuse*. Colorado Springs, CO: Nav Press, 2008.

   Sexual abuse knows no religious or social boundaries. The Wounded Heart is an intensely personal and specific look at this form of abuse. Dr. Allender explores the secret lament of the soul damaged by sexual abuse and lays hold of the hope buried there by the One whose unstained image we all bear. (Workbook also available – useful in church support groups for survivors)

2. Bass, Ellen and Laura . *The Courage to Heal 4e: A Guide for Women Survivors of Child Sexual Abuse*. New York: William Morrow Publishing, 2008. (Workbook also available)

   The Courage to Heal is an inspiring, comprehensive guide that offers hope and a map of the healing journey to every woman who was sexually abused as a child—and to those who care about her. Although the effects of child sexual abuse are long-term and severe, healing is possible.

3. Heggen, Carolyn Holderread. Sexual Abuse in Christian Homes and Churches. Eugene, OR: Wipf & Stock Publishers, 2006

What sets this book apart from the many others on the topic is the emphasis on how a church congregation can begin to work to heal the wounds of sexual abuse and prevent further abuses from happening. Church members often must, at the same time, offer love, under-standing, and healing to survivors while confronting (and still loving) the perpetrator.

4. Heitritter, Lynn and Jeanette Vought. *Helping Victims of Sexual Abuse: A Sensitive Biblical Guide for Counselors, Victims and Families.* Bloomington, MN: Bethany House Publishers, 2006.

   This solidly biblical and sensitive guide is packed full of helpful infor-mation that provides a valuable perspective on how abuse affects chil-dren and the family dynamics that play into its development. As well, readers will also discover practical tools that can lead adult victims into full recovery in Christ. Required reading for everyone who wants to bring meaningful ministry to those affected by sexual abuse.

5. Lew, Mike. Victims No Longer: *The Classic Guide for Men Recovering from Sexual Child Abuse.* New York: Harper Perennial, 2004.

   The first book written specifically for men, Victims No Longer exam-ines the changing cultural attitudes toward male survivors of incest and other sexual trauma. Now, in this Second Edition, this invaluable resource continues to offer compassionate and practical advice, sup-ported by personal anecdotes and statements of male survivors.

PTSD

1. Orange, Cynthia. Shock Waves: *A Practical Guide to Living with a Loved One's PTSD.* Center City, MN: Hazelden, 2010

   A practical, user-friendly guide for those who love someone whose life has been changed by trauma, whether or not that person has been diagnosed with PTSD. Throughout its pages are the voices of trauma survivors and those affected by a loved one's trauma.

2. Williams, Mary Beth and Soili Poijula. *The PTSD Workbook: Simple, Effective Techniques for Overcoming Traumatic Stress Symptoms.* Oakland, CA: New Harbinger Publications, 2002

In The PTSD Workbook, two psychologists and trauma experts gather together techniques and interventions used by PTSD experts from around the world to offer trauma survivors the most effective tools available to conquer their most distressing trauma-related symptoms. Readers learn how to determine the type of trauma they experienced, identify their symptoms, and learn the most effective strategies they can use to overcome them.

Domestic Violence

1. Alsdurf, James and Phyllis. Battered into Submission: The Tragedy of Wife Abuse in the Christian Home. Downers Grove, IL: InterVarsity Press, 1998

2. Kroeger, Catherine Clark and Nancy Nason-Clark. *No Place for Abuse: Biblical and Practical Resources to Counteract Domestic Violence.* Downers Grove, IL: InterVarsity Press, 2010.

   The authors demonstrate that the problem of domestic violence in the church is more pervasive than most Christians would like to believe. This thought-provoking book has the potential to open the eyes of many believers who don't understand the prevalence of violence in many evangelical homes. It will be particularly useful to pastors and counselors, but will offer guidance to any Christian who has encountered such situations.

Endnotes

1. U.S. Department of Health and Human Services. Administration for Children and Families. *Child Maltreatment Report*, 2011. www.acf.hhs.gov/programs/cb/resource/child-maltreatment-2011
2. United States Government Accountability Office, Report to the Chairman, Committee on Ways and Means, House of Representatives. *Child Mistreatment*, July 2011. www.gao.gov/new.items/d11599.pdf
3. D. Finkelhor et al., "Sexual Abuse in a National Survey of Adult Men and Women: Prevalence, Characteristics, and Risk Factors," *Child Abuse and Neglect*, no. 14 (1990):19-28.
4. D. W. Smith et al., "Delay in Disclosure of Childhood Rape: Results from a National Survey," *Child Abuse & Neglect*, (2000): 24.
5. Patricia Tjaden & Nancy Thoennes, "Extent, Nature and Consequences of Intimate Partner Violence," *The National Violence against Women Survey*, (2000): 9-10. https://www.ncjrs.gov/pdffiles1/nij/181867.pdf
6. Tjaden, 12-13.
7. Callie Rennison, "Intimate Partner Violence, 1993-2001," *Bureau of Justice Statistics Crime Data Brief*, no.197838 (2003). http://bjs.ojp.usdoj.gov/content/pub/pdf/ipv01.pdf
8. Irene Frieze and Angela Browne, "Violence in Marriage," *Crime and Justice* 11, (1989):163-218.
9. A. R. Roberts, *Battered Women and their Families*. (NY: Springer Publishing, 1992), 147-167.
10. Freedictionary.com, s. v. "victim," accessed October 14, 2012, www.thefreedictionary.com/victim
11. Freedictionary.com, s. v. "survivor," accessed October 14, 2012, www.thefreedictionary.com/survivor

12. D. Campbell et al., "Cycle of child sexual abuse: links between being a victim and becoming a perpetrator." *The British Journal of Psychiatry* (2001): 482-494.

13. Andrew Vachss, "You Carry the Cure in your Heart," Parade Magazine, August 28, 1994.

14. Melinda Smith and Jeanne Segal, "Child Abuse and Neglect: Recognizing and Preventing Child Abuse," Last modified November, 2012. http://www.helpguide.org/mental/child_abuse_physical_emotional_sexual_neglect.htm

15. Allender, Dan, *The Wounded Heart: Hope for Adult Victims of Childhood Sexual Abuse.* (CO: Nav Press, 1990), 79-83.

16. Medical-dictionary.thefreedictionary.com, s. v. "debridement," accessed November 10, 2012, http://medical-dictionary.thefreedictionary.com/debridement

17. William Worden, *Grief Counseling and Grief Therapy: A Handbook for Mental Health Practitioners*, NY: Springer Publishing, 1982

18. Henry Cloud and John Townsend, *Boundaries: When to Say Yes, When to Say No, to Take Control of Your Life*, Grand Rapids, MI: Zondervan, 1992.

19. Nina W. Brown, *Coping With Infuriating, Mean, Critical People - The Destructive Narcissistic Pattern*, Westport, CN: Praeger Publishing, 2006.

20. Lewis B. *Smedes, Forgive* or Forget: Healing the Hurts We *Don't Deserve*, (New York: HarperOne, 2007), 111.

21. www.christiansurvivors.com/forgiveness.html, accessed November 3, 2012.

22. Smedes, 133.

23. U.S. Department of Health and Human Services, Administration for Children and Families, "Child Abuse and Neglect," 2008, https://www.childwelfare.gov/can/

24. U.S. Department of Justice Office on Violence against Women, "Domestic Violence", last modified August, 2012, www.ovw.usdoj.gov/domviolence.htm

25. Howard N. Snyder, "Sexual Assault of Young Children as Reported to Law Enforcement: Victim, Incident, and Offender Characteristics," National Center for Juvenile Justice, July, 2000, http://www.ojp.usdoj.gov/bjs

26. Ronald and Stephen Holmes, *Profiling Violent Crimes: An Investigative Tool*, (Thousand Oaks, CA: Sage Publications, 2002), 3-12.

27. G.G. Abel, M. S. Mittelman and J. V. Becker, "Sexual Offenders: Results of Assessment and Recommendations for Treatment," *Clinical*

Criminology: The Assessment and Treatment of Criminal Behavior (Toronto: M & M Graphics, 1985), 191-205.

28. J. Caffaro and A. Conncaffaro, "Treating Sibling Abuse Families," *Aggression and Violent Behavior* no. 10 (2005): 604.

29. Child Protection Guide, 3rd edition. www.childprotectionguide.org/ child-protection-eguide-subjects/a-child-molesters-confession

30. Angela R. Carl, *Child Abuse: What You Can Do About It*, (Cincinnati, OH: Standard Pub, 1985).

31. Jordan and Margaret Paul, *Do I Have to Give Up Me to Be Loved by You Workbook*. (MN: Hazelden, 2002), p. 65

32. www.ptsd.va.gov/public/understanding_ptsd/booklet.pdf

33. www.helpguide.org/mental/domestic_violence_abuse_types_signs_ causes_effects.htm

34. Frequently Asked Questions about Domestic Violence. National Network to End Domestic Violence, 2010. www.nnedv.org/docs/Stats/ NNEDV_FAQaboutDV2010.pdf

35. Lenore E. Walker, A. *The Battered Woman Syndrome*, 3rd ed. (NY: Springer Publishing Company, 2009), 98-101.

36. New Hampshire Coalition against Domestic and Sexual Violence. "Faith Based Issues and Domestic Violence" www.nhcadsv.org/ DVFaith_Based_Issues.cfm

37. Brenda Branson and Paula Silva. "Violence Among Believers: Confronting the Destructive Secret," *Christian Counseling Today*, no. 13:3, (2005), 24-27.

38. Frequently Asked Questions about Domestic Violence. National Network to End Domestic Violence, 2010. www.nnedv.org/docs/Stats/ NNEDV_FAQaboutDV2010.pdf

39. Women's Health.gov Sexual Assault Fact Sheet, 2009. www.women-shealth.gov/publications/our-publications/fact-sheet/sexual-assault. cfm

About the Author

*R*oberta Fish, LCSW, received her MSW from the University of IL at Chicago and attended Northern Baptist Theological Seminary, Lombard, IL.

She has served God through a variety of careers: registered nurse, pastor's wife, business entrepreneur, psychotherapist, campus chaplain, professor of religion and psychology, pastor, retreat/seminar leader and author.

Encouraging people to learn and grow has been her lifelong ministry. She has practiced psychotherapy over thirty years supporting clients in their work of healing.

Eighteen years ago, Roberta and Juanita Mayer-Bartel created Hope for Hurting Hearts, a supportive educational retreat week-end for women with abuse issues. She and Juanita have facilitated this retreat nationally numerous times.

Roberta Fish lives in central Florida with her husband of 46 years who, she says, is the kindest man she knows and her biggest cheerleader. She has three amazing red-headed sons, three lovely daughters-in-love, seven brilliant grandchildren and five darling great-grandsons. In her "down time" she loves playing the piano, singing, biking, doing cross stitch, playing dominoes (with her husband) and reading.

Her second book will be published the end of 2013; a readable inspirational Bible commentary on the gospel women, entitled The Good News Women.

www.robertafish.com
www.hopeforhurtinghearts.com

CPSIA information can be obtained at www.ICGtesting.com
Printed in the USA
BVOW062047030213

312232BV00003B/10/P

9 781625 093219